ARCHAEOLOGICAL INVESTIGATIONS IN THE SOUTHERN HIEROGLYPHIC MOUNTAINS, MARICOPA COUNTY, ARIZONA

by

DONALD R. KELLER
ARTHUR W. VOKES
DARBI M. REA

with contributions by

SUZANNE K. FISH
LISA W. HUCKELL
LINDA J. PIERCE

SWCA, Inc.
Environmental Consultants
Flagstaff

SWCA Anthropological Research Paper Number 6

1998

General series editor - Robert C. Euler
Assistant editor - Richard V. N. Ahlstrom
Copy editors - Sally P. Bennett and Jean H. Ballagh
Cover design - Christina Watkins

SWCA, Inc., Environmental Consultants
1998

ISBN 1 – 931901 – 10 – 4

TABLE OF CONTENTS

List of Figures

List of Tables

ABSTRACT

Archaeologists from SWCA, Inc., Environmental Consultants, studied seven small archaeological sites located in the Hieroglyphic Mountains of Maricopa County, Arizona, as a requirement of a proposed exchange of U.S. Bureau of Land Management (BLM) land from public to private ownership. Inventory and study of affected cultural resources is a federally mandated part of the exchange process aimed at mitigating possible adverse effects to the sites prior to completion of the exchange.

SWCA conducted the data recovery program (BLM Project No. BLM-020-14-88-181) during the spring of 1988 under contract to Headquarters West, Ltd. The investigated sites are located in Section 5, Township 5 North, Range 1 West, and Sections 27, 31, 34, and 35, Township 6 North, Range 1 West (USGS 7.5 minute Baldy Mountain, Arizona, and Hieroglyphic Mountains, Arizona, quadrangles).

Investigated sites include five prehistoric and protohistoric camp and work sites and two historic mine sites. Two of the aboriginal sites contained small rockshelters with substantial cultural deposits. Data recovery activities included site mapping, surface artifact collection, and subsurface testing and excavation.

Prehistoric Hohokam components dated to the Colonial, Sedentary, and Classic periods (A.D. 700–1450). Yavapai components, present at two sites, may span the period from A.D. 1300 to 1700 or even later; some ethnographic evidence was present for use into historic times. Both Hohokam and Yavapai use of the area appeared to have related to seasonal gathering of wild-plant foods, primarily saguaro and other cacti, leguminous-tree seed pods, and possibly greens and grass seeds, and exploitation of animal resources, particularly deer, rabbit, and tortoise.

The historic mine sites appeared to have been small-scale operations. They were in use during several time periods including the late 1800s, the World War I era, the 1920s, and the 1950s. Gold was probably the mineral of interest; copper was also present.

CHAPTER 1

PROJECT BACKGROUND AND RESEARCH DESIGN

Donald R. Keller

This document presents descriptions, analyses, and interpretations of data recovered during investigations at seven archaeological sites in the Hieroglyphic Mountains of central Arizona (Figure 1.1). The sites are among 13 recorded during a sample survey of 8385 acres of U.S. Department of the Interior, Bureau of Land Management (BLM) land southwest of Lake Pleasant, in Section 5, Township 5 North, Range 1 West, and Sections 27, 31, 34, and 35, Township 6 North, Range 1 West, in the USGS 7.5 minute Baldy Mountain and Hieroglyphic Mountains, Arizona, quadrangles (Figure 1.2) (Greenwald and Keller 1988a). The archaeological survey and subsequent excavations were conducted in conjunction with the exchange of these lands from federal to private ownership and in conformance with federal requirements for mitigation of impacts to cultural resources.

BACKGROUND

In 1988 Headquarters West, Ltd., contracted with SWCA, Inc., Environmental Consultants, to perform a cultural resource inventory of the land to be exchanged and a subsequent data recovery program at four prehistoric sites and two historic sites, as described in the project research design (Greenwald and Keller 1988b). A seventh site was discovered during data recovery and added to the project. Two of the prehistoric sites were small rockshelters with interior cultural deposits and associated artifact scatters. The other two prehistoric sites consisted of artifact scatters with features of limited depth; a third artifact scatter was examined as well. Both Hohokam and protohistoric Yavapai components were represented. The two historic sites were small shaft and tunnel mines with associated camp remains representing Euroamerican culture. The research topics to which the sites contributed information included site function, temporal and cultural relationships, environment and subsistence, and group size.

SWCA carried out the data recovery program (BLM Project No. BLM-020-14-88-181) between May 16 and June 4, 1988, under BLM Cultural Resource Use Permit AZ-000008. The work included detailed mapping, controlled surface artifact collection, subsurface excavation, photodocumentation, and pollen, macrobotanical, and radiocarbon sampling. Staff at SWCA's laboratory in Tucson processed the project collections; personnel at SWCA facilities in Tucson and Flagstaff performed the analyses. Materials and data were curated at the Arizona State Museum (ASM). All assigned site numbers were ASM designations; Table 1.1 lists the equivalent BLM numbers.

Table 1.1. Arizona State Museum (ASM) and Bureau of Land Management (BLM) Site Numbers

ASM Site No.	BLM Site No.
AZ T:3:41	AZ T:3:1
AZ T:3:42	AZ T:3:2
AZ T:3:43	AZ T:3:3
AZ T:3:45	AZ T:3:5
AZ T:3:46	AZ T:3:15
AZ T:3:48	AZ T:3:6
AZ T:3:52	AZ T:3:17

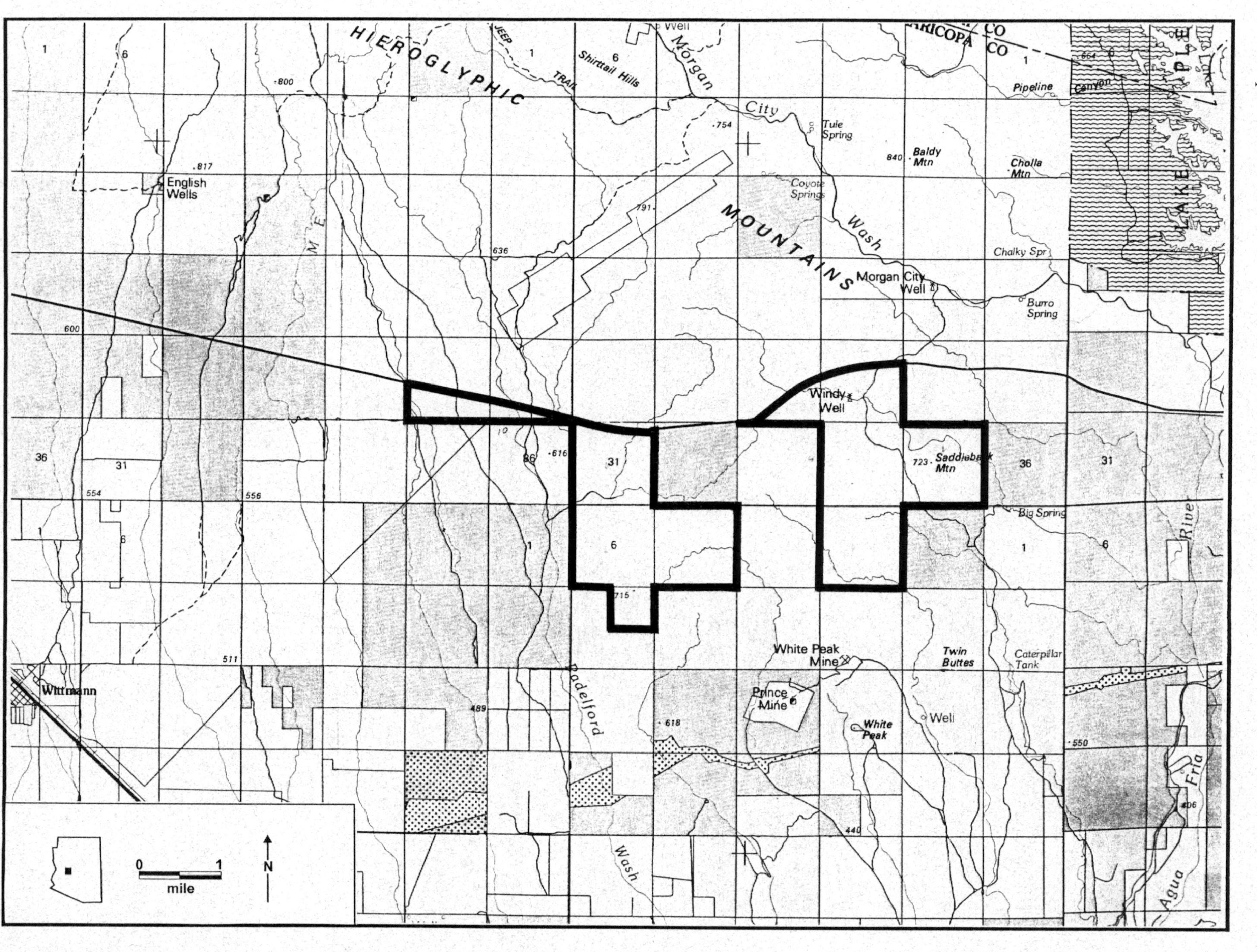

Figure 1.1. Location of project area in southeastern Hieroglyphic Mountains. Base map is BLM 1:100,000 scale series Phoenix North, Arizona (1979).

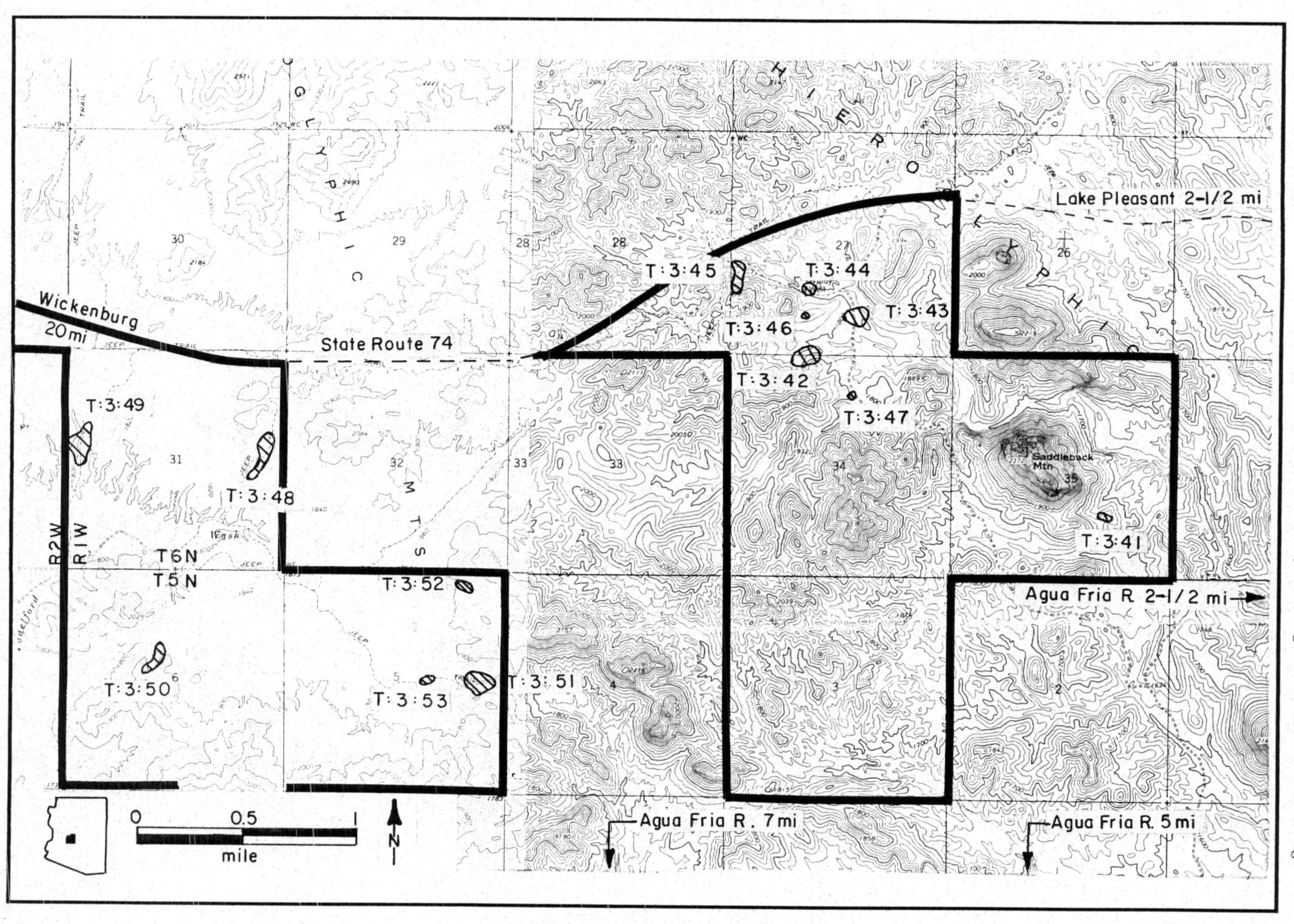

Figure 1.2. Location of project sites. Base maps are Hieroglyphic Mountains SW and Baldy Mountain, Arizona, USGS 7.5′ series (photorevised 1981).

Environment and Physiography

The project sites were in the southern end of the Hieroglyphic Mountains at elevations ranging from 1780 feet to 1900 feet (545–580 m) above sea level. This upland desert landscape is composed of rocky hills interspersed with minor alluvial benches along drainages and in small valleys. All local drainages eventually flow into the Agua Fria River. The major drainage in the western portion of the project area is Padelford Wash. In the eastern project area, a number of steeper, unnamed washes run directly into the Agua Fria between Lake Pleasant and Calderwood Butte. The most prominent landmark in the area is Saddleback Mountain with an elevation of 2372 feet (723 m).

The substrate in the project area consists primarily of metamorphic and volcanic rock types or colluvial and alluvial deposits derived from them. Just east of the project area lies the edge of an upper bajada that extends westward to the Hassayampa River and south to the White Tank Mountains.

Modern average annual precipitation in the southern Hieroglyphic Mountains appears to be just over 254 mm (10 inches). Annual rainfall extremes reported for the area range from lows of 83.8–190.5 mm (3.3–7.5 inches) to highs of 375.9–779.8 mm (14.8-30.7 inches) (Sellers and Hill 1974).

Surface water is not common in the project area, although field personnel observed water at the spring at Site AZ T:3:42(ASM). Not surprisingly, this water was more abundant during the survey in February than during the excavations in June. Four other springs exist within a three-mile radius of Site AZ T:3:42(ASM). Three of these, Burro, Chalky, and Big Springs, are within reasonable walking distance of the project area. The Agua Fria River, three miles east of the project area and 400 feet lower in elevation, is in places a perennial stream (Brown, Carmony, and Turner 1979). Other potential water sources include a number of wash-bottom bedrock catchment holes that probably contain water during some seasons in particularly moist years.

Vegetation in the project area represents the Arizona Upland subdivision of the Sonoran Desertscrub formation, Paloverde–Cacti–Mixed Scrub series (Turner and Brown 1982), the best watered and least desert-like of North American desertscrub areas. The series is characterized by an open scrubland or low woodland dominated by foothill paloverde, saguaro, ironwood, honey mesquite, catclaw and white thorn acacia, creosotebush, bursage, ocotillo, and several *Opuntia* cacti. An abundant understory of grasses and annuals exists in places during wet periods of the year. Some of these species, such as *Plantago* (plantain), undoubtedly had potential economic value for prehistoric peoples in the region.

The present regional environment is no more than 8000–9000 years old (Turner and Brown 1982). Prior to that time, the area probably supported woodland vegetation including juniper, piñon, oak, and sage in communities similar to modern plant associations found several thousand feet higher in elevation. Within the last 100–120 years, ranching and mining have, to some extent, altered the area's physical aspect. In particular, cattle have caused serious soil and groundcover disturbance within the project area.

Cultural Context

Paleoindian and Archaic Periods

Evidence for Paleoindian and Archaic period occupation of the Hieroglyphic Mountains and adjacent areas is limited. Only one Paleoindian projectile point has been reported for the region (Huckell 1982). Evidence of subsequent Archaic use includes components in the Interstate 17–New River Interchange area (Rice and Dobbins 1981), the Deer Valley area (Ferg 1977), and an excavated site near San Domingo Wash (AZ T:2:1[ASM]) (Rice and Dobbins 1981). On the basis of projectile point style, Rice and Dobbins assigned the latter site to the late Archaic San Pedro phase of the Cochise tradition (ca. 1000 B.C. – A.D. 1). West of Wickenburg, Keller (1986) recorded an extensive late Archaic base camp on upper Centennial Wash. Green (1989) also recorded three possible Archaic sites in the New River area for the Waddell Project. One site (AZ T:4:40[ASM]) had two roasting pits, another site (AZ T:4:43[ASM]) had a roasting pit and a projectile point that possibly dated to the Archaic, and a third site (AZ T:4:44[ASM]) had a single roasting pit. In all cases, the dates obtained were from samples removed from the roasting pits (Green 1989:1068).

These data suggest a limited use of the area immediately north of the Phoenix Basin, or possibly that most sites from the Archaic period have yet to be investigated. The New River area appears to be an exception and may well have supported a larger Archaic population. Thus far, however, the data suggest that occupation was probably restricted to the terminal Archaic San Pedro phase, after 1000 B.C. (Stone 1986). With the possible exception of one projectile point (Chapter 4), SWCA's investigators found no direct evidence of Archaic period use of the Hieroglyphic Mountains study area.

Hohokam Occupation

The Hohokam tradition dates to approximately A.D. 150–1450 (Wilcox and Shenk 1977). The subsistence base incorporated a number of agricultural techniques ranging from rock-terrace rainfall farming to complex canal irrigation. Evidence of the dietary importance of wild plant foods is also found at many Hohokam settlements (Gasser 1980). Factors affecting the relative importance of domesticated plant foods and cultivated or gathered wild food may have been natural or cultural or both. Possible natural influences are the nature and stability of prevailing climatic regimes and the accessibility of wild food resources. Cultural factors may have included the success rate and nutritional potential of particular farming methods, pressures placed on developed farming areas, competition for wild food resources, and the nature and development of intra- and intergroup exchange networks.

Hohokam use of the Hieroglyphic Mountains study area appears to have been associated with the northward expansion of Hohokam populations from the core area along the Salt and Gila rivers into drainages originating in the central Arizona highlands (Gumerman and Spoerl 1980; Wilcox and Sternberg 1983). Occupation of this northern periphery appears to have been permanent or semipermanent by A.D. 700 (Weaver 1980).

Although ceramic evidence suggests that the area was used by Hohokam groups on a temporary basis as early as A.D. 500, the most intensive occupation occurred during the Santa Cruz and Sacaton phases (A.D. 700–1100). Santa Cruz and Sacaton Red-on-buff pottery dominate assemblages of decorated ceramics (Henderson and Rodgers 1979; Howard 1989; Rodgers 1987), with varying amounts of earlier Snaketown and Gila Butte Red-on-buff and later Casa Grande Red-on-buff. Sacaton and Gila Red are present in the area, with Gila Plain and Wingfield Plain dominant in the New River, Calderwood Butte, and Cave Creek areas, at least after A.D. 800. Decorated wares in the area include a sand-tempered variety with frequent smudging (Greenwald 1988; Weaver 1980).

Although the northern periphery was largely depopulated by A.D. 1100–1150, Weaver (1980) reported documentation of Hohokam trails used as late as A.D. 1300 in the Agua Fria and New River areas. Several sites on Cave Creek and New River showed evidence of agricultural use until about A.D. 1200 or 1250 (Rodgers 1987).

With the exception of rockshelters and limited activity sites, Hohokam sites are typically found on low terraces along major drainages and their tributaries. These sites contain structural remains and are associated with arable soils and small-scale irrigation, floodwater, and rainfall farming features (Ranken and Katzer 1989; Rodgers 1987; Weaver 1980).

Excavated sites in the vicinity of the project area include the Beardsley Canal Site (Weed 1972), Calderwood Ruin (Dove 1970), and a rockshelter site (AZ T:3:16[ASM]) southwest of Lake Pleasant (Gumerman, Weed, and Hanson 1976). Other excavated sites include the Westwing (Weaver 1974) and Eastwing sites (Rodgers 1987) on the Agua Fria, the Baccharis site (Greenwald 1988), and sites in the New River Dam Archaeological District (Doyel 1984), all located on the New River drainage. The Waddell Project, south and southeast of Lake Pleasant, included excavation of 17 sites in the Agua Fria and New River borrow areas (Green 1989). In addition, Ayres (1967) excavated one site on Cave Creek in the Paradise Valley Archaeological Complex. Green (1986) has provided a comprehensive review of previous survey and excavation work in the Agua Fria area.

Macrobotanical and palynological studies at a number of sites in the Hohokam northern periphery indicate subsistence use of a number of domesticated and wild plant species (Bohrer 1984; Henderson and Rodgers 1979; Rodgers 1987; Ruppé 1988). Identified cultivars include maize and possibly Cheno-am species, squash, and cotton. Gathered wild species include mesquite, globemallow, purslane, Mormon tea, mustard, prickly pear, grasses, spiderling, Liguliflorae, and probably saguaro, chenopods, and amaranths. Documentation also indicates that prehistorically exploited faunal resources in the Agua Fria and adjacent areas include rabbit, hare, deer, bighorn sheep, pronghorn, coyote, fox, bobcat, and desert tortoise.

Green (1986, 1989), Greenwald (1988), Henderson and Rodgers (1979), Rodgers (1987), and Spoerl and Gumerman (1984) have discussed considerations of local adaptation and chronology, local and inter-drainage relations, and regional interaction, all research domains relevant to study of the Hohokam northern periphery. The data collected during the present study have contributed to better understanding of economic diversity, wild resource exploitation, seasonality, and chronology.

Protohistoric Period

The first European known to have encountered the Yavapai was the Spanish explorer Antonio Espejo, in the Verde Valley in A.D. 1583. Some researchers believe that Yavapai entry into the region, which appears to date to A.D. 1300 or later, is related to a relatively late expansion of Yuman groups out of the lower Colorado River area (Pilles 1981). The Yavapai remained relatively undisturbed by Euroamerican expansion until the 1860s (Greenwald and Keller 1988a; Pilles 1981).

The project area is in what was probably the south-central margin of the protohistoric Yavapai range. At the time of historic contact, the relatively sedentary Maricopa and Pima occupied the broad desert valleys of the Salt and Gila rivers to the south. Friendly relations apparently obtained between these groups and the Yavapai until the period between 1689 and 1746, when the Apache entered central Arizona (Schroeder 1974). According to Gifford (1936), an unoccupied buffer zone subsequently existed between the Yavapai and the Pima and Maricopa as a result of hostilities between them. Prior to this time, the Yavapai may have foraged somewhat farther south than their documented protohistoric range, and the present project area may have been within or near the buffer zone during portions of the protohistoric period.

The Yavapai based their subsistence strategy on a yearly round of nomadic foraging and limited cultivation. The small amount of agriculture they practiced probably had only minimal effect on the scheduling of wild plant gathering. Maize was planted at 4400 feet (1342 m) along Big Bug Creek in June, undoubtedly well before the saguaro harvest, then left largely unattended until it was ripe (Gifford 1936). According to Gifford (1936), the ripening of saguaro fruit in mid June was an annual event that attracted the Yavapai to the low-lying parts of their territory, including the project area. Leguminous seed pods such as those of the mesquite, paloverde, and ironwood were gathered in conjunction with the saguaro harvest. The timing of the pod harvest was probably less critical than that of the saguaro, since pods can be processed for consumption at various stages of ripening.

During July, the Northeastern Yavapai returned to upland locations in the area of Mayer, Arizona, 45–50 miles north of the project area. They spent late summer and fall in higher altitudes gathering acorns, walnuts, piñon nuts, and other seeds. They gathered agave in early summer in upland areas east of Mayer and collected various greens in the spring.

The staple meat of the Yavapai was venison, and they hunted deer in hilly country in all seasons. They also ate pronghorn, mountain sheep, rabbit, woodrat, squirrel, coyote, mountain lion, wildcat, fox, ring-tail cat, badger, porcupine, skunk, dog, chuckwalla, desert tortoise, numerous bird species including dove, quail, and turkey, and a large species of caterpillar. Some of these, including the tortoise, they cooked by slow baking in a small earth oven. They cracked deer long bones and ate the marrow raw (Gifford 1936:265).

Historic Period

Historic period activities in the project area have been largely limited to small-scale ranching and mining. Arizona Department of Mines and Mineral Resources (ADMMR) archives list gold and copper mines both within and adjacent to the project area (Dosh 1989). The H. J. Bennett (Arizona–Buffalo) Mine, in the NW¼ of the SE¼ of Section 5, dates to the 1890s. The company abandoned the associated shaft and structures in the first half of this century.

Archival research at the BLM and ADMMR yielded little information concerning project area sites. At ADMMR, 1997 mining district maps for Maricopa County show Site AZ T:3:48(ASM) as containing "unknown shaft and prospect 1." A check of the General Land Office (GLO), Master Title Plats (MTP), and MTP Historic Indexes for this site produced no information. For Site AZ T:3:45(ASM), the GLO records indicate a mine shaft at this location by December of 1941; the MTP indicates that the mine shaft was within lot 9 of this section. Further research discovered no date for the subdivision and no homestead or mining claim patents for the lot or section, and Mining District Survey Plats at the BLM contain no district claims for this section. The ADMMR 1997 mining district maps for Maricopa County identify the site as "unknown shaft 9."

The project area is within and adjacent to the Pikes Peak Mining District (Johnson 1972:26, Plate 1). The Pikes Peak Mining District, also known as the Morgan City Mining District (Arizona State Bureau of Mines 1961:61) is a gold placer district centered on Morgan City Wash, south of the Maricopa County Line on the west side of the Agua Fria. The wash was named after the Morgan City Mine, located one township north of the project area (Granger 1983:421). The mine was named after its founder, Pat Morgan, a prospector who located rich gold ore in the vicinity in 1874 (Granger 1983:421). The Arizona State Bureau of Mines (1961:58) lists the total gold production for the Pikes Peak Mining District as $490 for the years 1939–1948 and the total production for Maricopa County as $40,108 in the years 1932–1949. Johnson (1972:26) reports no other records for gold production in the Pikes Peak Mining District, noting that it is known for its iron deposits.

Roughly 18 miles west of the project area and the Pikes Peak Mining District is the better-known Vulture Mining District, named after the important Vulture Mine. This mine followed the typical pattern of boom and bust for most mines. The Vulture Mine was discovered by Henry Wickenburg in 1863 and in the early days of its operation provided easy wealth (McClintock 1916:404). The Vulture Mine is considered to have been one of the most productive gold mines in the Southwest. Some reports put the total output of the mine near $10,000,000, but more reliable reports indicate that, at least for the first six years of operation, output was nearer $2,500,000 (McClintock 1916:404–405). Between 1864 and 1865, as many as 40 arrastras processed the ore from the Vulture Mine. The arrastras were superseded by two small mills in 1865, which were later replaced by bigger mills. One of the first two mills was built by Michael Goldwater, who extracted gold worth $3000 per day before selling the mill when the quality of the ore took a precipitous fall (McClintock 1916:404). In 1866, B. Phelps bought the main claim of the Vulture Mining Company, and in 1867 the output of the mine was only $45,633. Up to roughly 1880, recovery of large nuggets of gold was not uncommon at the Vulture Mine. Most of the large nuggets weighed between one-half ounce and one ounce, but some weighed as much as five ounces (Johnson 1972:21). At this point, most of the richest gravels at the Vulture Mine had been worked out, although small-scale drywashing in the vicinity continued until 1948 (Johnson 1972:21).

Although the Spanish were raising cattle along what is now the Arizona–New Mexico border in the seventeenth century, Euroamericans seem to have made the first attempts at cattle ranching in central and northern Arizona in the 1860s, when three herds were reported "near Prescott" (Haskett 1935). Accounts of the time relate that in many areas of the Arizona Territory, including the triangle bounded by Wickenburg, Prescott, and Lake Pleasant, the native grasses grew abundantly and to considerable height. However, Apache and Yavapai raids defeated earlier nineteenth-century efforts to establish ranches, and the withdrawal of federal troops during the Civil War made ranching completely untenable. The return of the army and the subjugation of the native inhabitants in the early 1870s led to renewed efforts to introduce cattle raising, partly in order to feed both the troops and the captive tribes (Haskett 1935). It was the coming of the railroad in the early 1880s that finally made ranching feasible. In the 1890s W. H. Beardsley developed an irrigation scheme to bring homesteaders into the area; the plan originally failed for lack of subscribers but was ultimately realized when Waddell Dam was completed in 1927 (Green and Effland 1985). Archaeological records show no remains of irrigation or water diversion devices in the immediate project area. Ranches existed along and to the west of the Agua Fria (Green and Effland 1985), but none seem to have been recorded in the immediate vicinity. The inference is that if cattle were present, they were running on the open range, as they are today.

RESEARCH DESIGN

The research design identified four main topics or problem domains—site function, cultural and temporal affiliation, environment and subsistence, and population size and composition—for the prehistoric and historic aboriginal sites and posed specific research questions within each problem domain. All but the questions on environment and subsistence pertained to the historic mining-related sites as well. Minor differences between the two sets of research problems are discussed below.

Site Function

A principal goal of the research was to define the function of the various sites. At both the prehistoric and historic aboriginal sites, relatively abundant ground stone and the absence of any materials that would suggest continuous, long-term use of the sites appeared to indicate resource exploitation. However, the specific activities carried out at the sites and therefore their specific functions remained to be determined. Although the historic Euroamerican sites clearly belonged to the general context of mining, their inhabitants certainly carried out a variety of more specific activities or functions as well. The goal for these sites was to discover as many of these specific functions as possible. The research questions were:

1. What range of activities do the cultural materials and features at each site represent?

2. Were sites or site components of similar cultural association and age produced by similar activities?

3. What was the intensity and duration of use for each site?

4. To what extent did function change through time?

The investigating team anticipated that a variety of data could be employed to address these questions. For instance, they expected that data from artifacts would provide information on the nature of the activities carried out at the sites and that archaeobotanical and faunal remains would shed light on the subsistence aspects of site function. Where structures were present, architectural attributes could provide insight into site function and the intensity and duration of site use.

Cultural and Temporal Affiliation

This problem domain concerned identification of the period of use of each site and the identity of the occupying group or groups. Preliminary assessment tentatively attributed the majority of the aboriginal remains to the Hohokam, but some ceramic materials indicated that later Yavapai Indians also made use of the area. Historic remains indicated that Euroamericans used the area primarily during the 1920s and 1930s. SWCA's investigators expected that examination of the material culture assemblages would (1) provide evidence that could be used to establish the identity of the peoples who used the project area, including, perhaps, groups other than Hohokam or Yavapai, and (2) provide more precise temporal control and perhaps reveal as-yet-unrecognized periods or phases of use. The following questions addressed the general problem of temporal and cultural affiliation:

1. What time periods and/or phases of occupation do the sites represent? What is the evidence for temporal assignment of the remains? What methods of dating apply?

2. What was the cultural identity of the group or groups that created each site? What evidence supports this identification?

Temporally and culturally diagnostic artifacts such as ceramics, projectile points, and glass and metal containers were a principal source of information on these questions. Field personnel also took radiocarbon samples (Appendix A) when appropriate materials were available. In contexts with stratified deposits, the excavators took care to recover and record the materials in a way that would distinguish different temporal and cultural units so that analysts could compare stratigraphic data with other data sets from the sites.

Environment and Subsistence

All of the sites under consideration appeared from the survey (Greenwald and Keller 1988a) to relate in one way or another to resource exploitation. For both the prehistoric and the historic sites, a further research goal was to determine the nature of the resources sought and the degree to which the natural environment might have influenced site location. Information already available on the historic mining sites was adequate to address this question, and the research design did not seek additional data. The questions designed to address this problem domain were:

1. What plant, animal, or other natural resources did occupants of the project area exploit?

2. For what purposes did occupants exploit resources, and what processing methods did they use?

3. What may be determined about the character of the natural environment during the periods or phases of occupation, and what aspects of the natural environment influenced aboriginal use of the area?

4. What botanical evidence exists to link site location with hydrologic features? What were the factors involved in determining site location (distribution of plant and animal resources, water, or other)?

SWCA's investigators used information from pollen (Appendix B), macrobotanical (Appendix C), and faunal (Appendix D) materials to address these questions. Plant and animal remains, especially those that were burned or otherwise altered, helped to determine what resources were important to inhabitants of the project area. Artifact assemblages were also informative in terms of strategies relating to on-site consumption or preparation of resources for storage and transportation to other locales.

Population Size and Composition

Although surface artifact density was not high at any of the sites, all sites showed some evidence of either structures or sheltered areas, and the size of these remains provided a basis for estimating the size of the social units at each site. Artifact density and diversity also provided insight into population size, particularly at the historic mining sites. Researchers used this information to assess function, subsistence, and the sociological aspects of each site. The following research questions were relevant to these issues:

1. What is the size and function of each structure, and what is the density of cultural materials at each site?

2. What was the nature of the social group or groups that occupied each site? Were social groups task-specific, or were family units present?

3. How do population sizes and social groups compare through time? Do patterns vary with site function, with the resources being exploited, or with other, as-yet-unidentified, factors?

The research team was not able to address some aspects of these questions because the sites did not yield adequate data. However, the builders of the structures had used them at least in part as habitations, and investigators were able to apply appropriate floor-area formulas for estimating population size. They were also able to assess and compare artifact densities and distributions as aids in generating population estimates.

CHAPTER 2

FIELD METHODS AND EXCAVATION RESULTS

Donald R. Keller

In general, the fieldwork followed the procedures outlined in the project research design (Greenwald and Keller 1988b): site mapping, plan and profile drawings of excavated features, photographing of sites and features in both 35-mm black-and-white print and color slide formats, systematic surface artifact collection, judgmental surface artifact collection, and excavation of selected site features. Field crews screened all excavated fill through 1/4-inch mesh to maximize recovery of artifacts and botanical and faunal materials and collected pollen, flotation, and charcoal samples from selected contexts. Appendixes A–D present the results of the botanical, faunal, and radiocarbon analyses. The excavation team made topographic maps of the four prehistoric sites using a plane table and alidade. The site descriptions below include specific procedures used at individual sites.

PREHISTORIC SITES

AZ T:3:41(ASM)

Site AZ T:3:41(ASM) was on a knoll top on the southeastern flank of Saddleback Mountain at an elevation of 1789 feet (545 m) above sea level (Figure 1.1). The knoll slopes to the east into drainages running directly into the Agua Fria River three miles to the east. This location commands a broad view eastward over the Agua Fria valley from the New River Mountains to the Phoenix area (Figure 2.1a).

Six features were clustered within a 10 × 15–m area immediately east of the knoll crest (Figure 2.2). A larger area measuring 30 × 70 m that extended downslope from the features contained a light scatter of flaked stone, ground stone, and ceramics. The six features included a large circular rock alignment, a segment of masonry wall rubble, three small rock clusters, and a small ash lens and rock cluster. Investigations subsequently determined that a vague rock alignment originally designated Feature 6 was noncultural.

The field crews conducted a 100% surface collection in all 5 × 5–m units around site features and in an area containing decorated ceramics at the eastern edge of the site (Figure 2.2). They obtained an overall 50% surface sample by collecting only the northeastern and southwestern quarters of the remaining staked 10 × 10–m units. They tested Features 1, 2, 4, 5, 6, and 7 for subsurface remains.

Feature 1 was a 1.8 × 3.6–m cluster of basalt rock that appeared to represent the remains of a slightly concave coursed-masonry wall aligned east-southeast. Originally the wall was probably about 1 m in height. Excavation of a trench across the rock cluster to a depth of 10 cm below ground surface indicated that the feature was built directly on the aboriginal ground surface. Lithics recovered near Feature 1 consisted of a large scraper plane, a chopper, core fragments and shatter, and unmodified flakes.

Feature 2 consisted of a circular rock alignment 3.0 m in diameter (Figure 2.1b). The field crew excavated this feature after clearing the north and south quarters of surface material. The feature had little

Figure 2.1a. Overview looking east from AZ T:3:41(ASM); New River Mountains in background.

Figure 2.1b. AZ T:3:41(ASM), Feature 2, before excavation, looking northwest; meter stick in center.

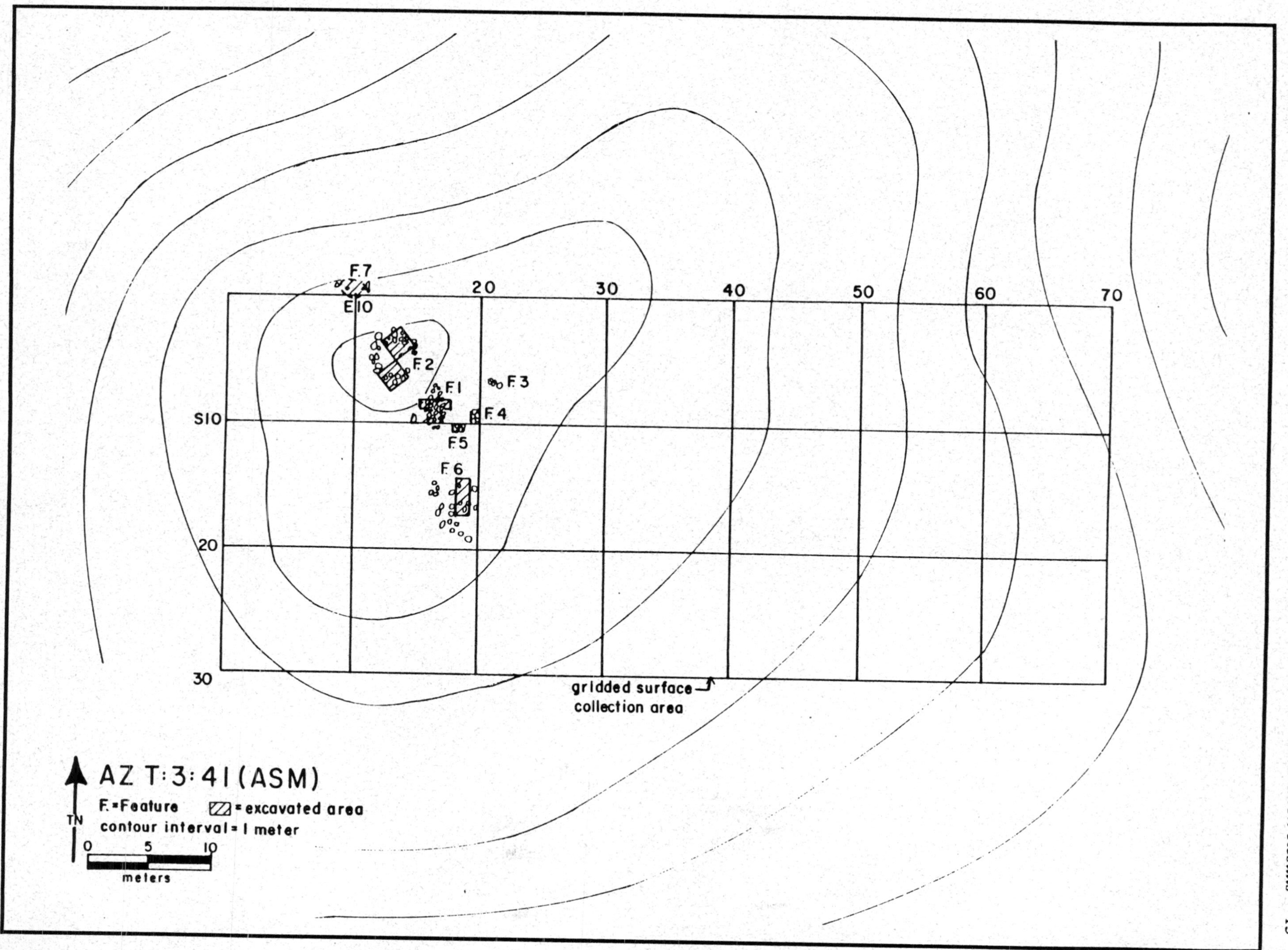

Figure 2.2. AZ T:3:41(ASM), site map.

or no depth, and the structural rocks lay directly on the aboriginal ground surface. Other than three quartz core and shatter pieces discovered immediately below surface level, the crew members encountered no subsurface cultural material. They excavated Feature 2 to a caliche horizon at a depth of 0.32 meters below datum (mbd), 7 cm below the modern ground surface.

The circular wall appeared to have been between one and three courses high and probably only a single course thick. A 1-m-wide break in the wall faced east-southeast. The apparently low wall height suggested that the feature was originally an anchor for a brush or pole superstructure. Excavators found no evidence of fire within the feature. Surface artifacts within the circle were a quartz core, shatter, flakes, and several sherds.

Features 3, 4, and 5 were small, irregular rock clusters measuring between 0.7 m and 1.0 m in diameter, each composed of between 7 and 10 rocks. Excavation of Features 4 and 5 revealed that the clusters were on the aboriginal ground surface. No appreciable cultural fill or artifacts were associated with these features. Excavation units were shallow, approximately 10 cm in depth. The features were aligned in a nearly straight line over a distance of 4.5 m. They may have served as supports for the upright posts of a shelter, shade, work frame, or drying rack.

Feature 7 was an irregular cluster of basalt rock on a slight bench near the top of the knoll. It measured 1.2 m in diameter and 13 cm in depth. A lens of ash and ash-stained soil approximately 60 cm in diameter was within the cluster. Feature 2 lay 4.0 m upslope from Feature 7. Burned soil underlying the ash layer and the presence of burned and fire-cracked rock indicated that this feature was a fire pit. Curiously, the fill contained no artifacts or other cultural materials.

AZ T:3:42(ASM)

Site AZ T:3:42(ASM) was in the bottom of a small valley northwest of Saddleback Mountain at an elevation of 1810 feet (552 m) (Figure 1.1). Within the site was a spring where a wash 4.0 m deep cuts through a geologic unit probably of Tertiary-age conglomerate (Kirk Anderson, personal communication 1988). Compared to most of the area's igneous bedrock, this unit appeared to be a superior aquifer. In addition, water dropping over the resistant conglomerate had created a relatively deep and protected catchment area undercutting the conglomerate ledge; water would have been available here much of the year (Greenwald and Keller 1988a).

The site included an artifact scatter and two small rockshelters immediately northeast of the spring along the south side of the wash (Figure 2.3). The artifact scatter covered a 70 × 190-m area on a relatively level terrace between the spring and a second wash to the north. Artifacts present included ceramics, flaked stone, and ground stone. Most of the artifacts were concentrated at the southwest end of the scatter near the base of a low hill. The gridded area shown in Figure 2.3 contained a fairly continuous artifact scatter. Single artifacts and small clusters were widely distributed over the rest of the flat, as indicated by the array of individual collection areas.

At this site the field crews conducted a 100% surface collection of 10 × 10-m units within a 30 × 50-m area encompassing the main artifact scatter (Figure 2.3). At other locations they made judgmental collections of individual artifacts and of artifacts within units 10 m in diameter. Shallow subsurface testing

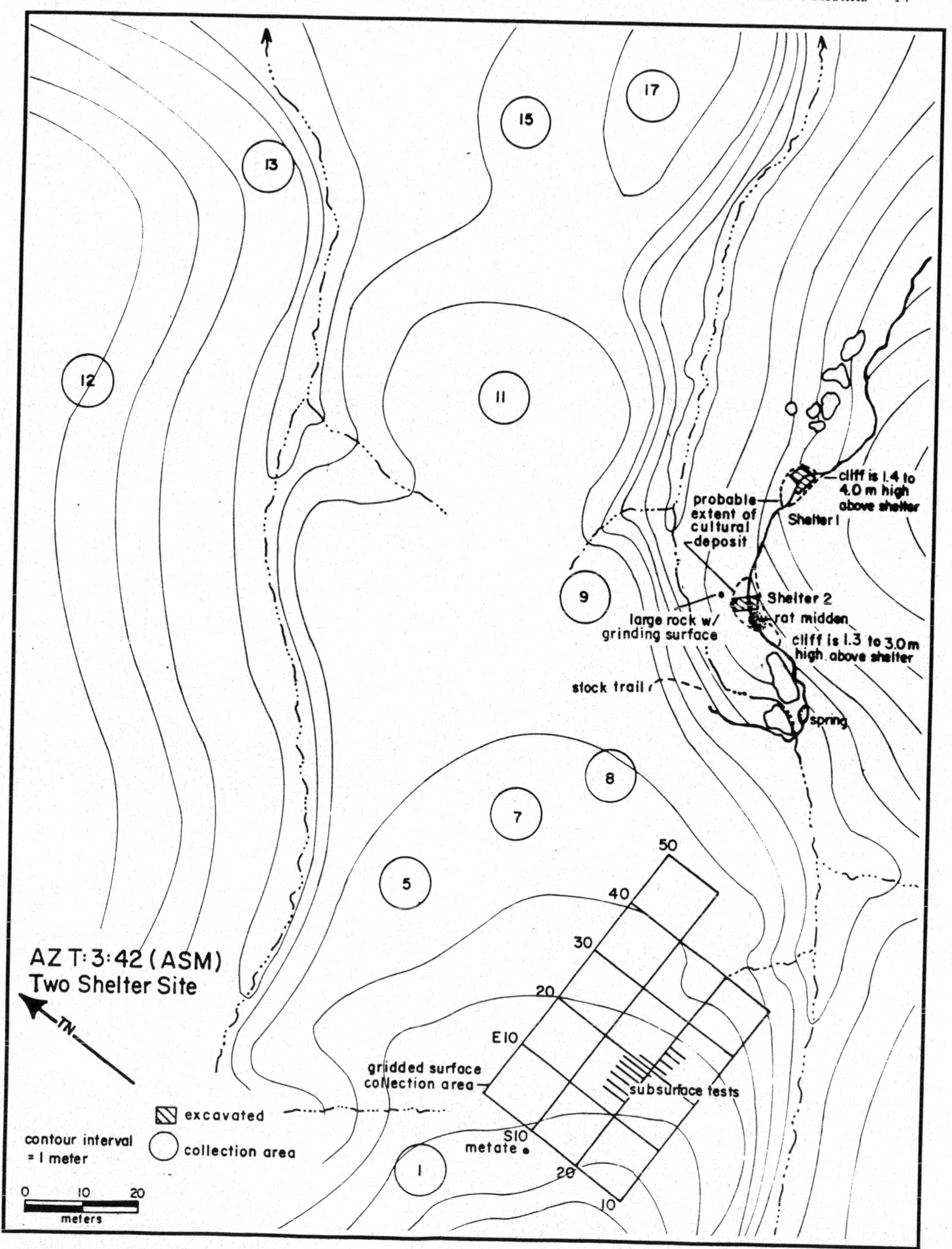

Figure 2.3. AZ T:3:42(ASM), site map.

to a depth of approximately 10 cm at the main artifact concentration and excavation of an area of apparently ash stained soil at S20, E20 (Figure 2.3) revealed no subsurface cultural deposits.

The crews excavated approximately half the cultural fill volume from within the two rockshelters: Shelter 1 to a maximum depth of 80 cm over an area of 10 m^2, and Shelter 2 to a maximum depth of 90 cm over an area of 8 m^2. They projected the innermost grid corners at both shelters vertically and inscribed them on the shelter ceilings for future reference.

Shelter 1

This small shelter consisted of a 4 × 9-m area of cultural deposition protected by a low overhanging cliff (Figure 2.4). The sheltered area averaged only 1.6 m in width along the cliff; consequently, the true dry shelter area was relatively small. No structural features or rock alignments were observed within the shelter. Much of the deposit consisted of natural roof fall occurring as small spalls. One particularly thick, continuous layer appeared to have collapsed during, or just prior to, site occupation. The shelter deposits were dry at the time of fieldwork, which would undoubtedly not be the case during particularly wet periods of the year.

A single stratum of cultural fill extending over the central and front part of the shelter averaged 25 cm in thickness but reached a depth of 40 cm at one point. This ashy gray fill was silty, with numerous pebble-sized rocks and abundant cultural material including charcoal flecks, lithics, bone, and ceramics. More perishable materials such as unburned wood were absent. The cultural fill was largely undifferentiated, especially in the front central portion of the shelter. Several lenses of very ashy material were recorded in the rear portions of the fill.

Deposition in the east half of the shelter was, in part, a product of colluvial slope wash entering from the east. At this end of the shelter, ashy cultural lenses interfaced with sloping layers of sterile colluvial material. Cultural deposits at the east edge of the shelter were covered by as much as 30 cm of sterile colluvium. Near the center of the shelter, 12 cm of sterile colluvium overlay a tongue of cultural fill. The colluvium graded to a silty cultural fill in the center and west parts of the shelter, where it varied between 5 cm and 12 cm in thickness. This deposit overlay the main body of cultural fill.

The layer of roof fall shown in Figure 2.4 underlay the main body of cultural fill. This layer, which was more or less continuous over most of the excavated shelter, was clearly sterile, although the roof fall included culturally stained or mixed fill. The roof-fall layer directly overlay an orange-colored sterile substrate that contained abundant pebble-sized rocks.

A lens of ash-stained brown-gray silt 8 cm thick underlay the roof fall in a limited area in the center of the shelter. Although it may have represented a cultural deposit that predated the roof fall, the lens is more likely the result of the downward movement of later cultural material originally deposited above the roof fall. This movement could have resulted from rodent disturbance or mechanical sifting. Data from the pollen analysis (Appendix B) also suggested that the roof-fall layer predated site occupation.

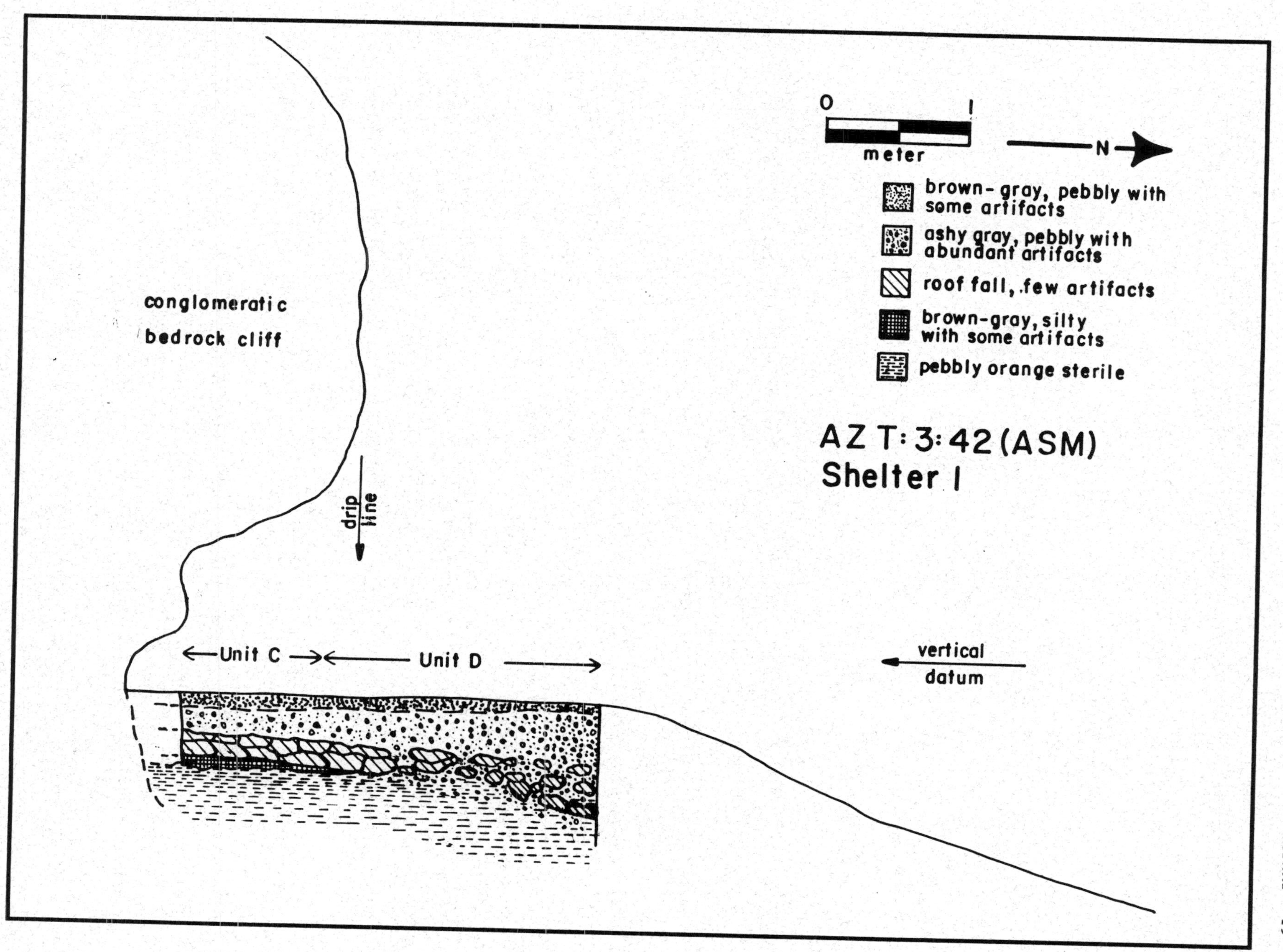

Figure 2.4. AZ T:3:42(ASM), Shelter 1 profile.

Shelter 2

This was a 4 × 8-m area partially sheltered by a rock overhang 2.0 m deep facing to the northwest (Figure 2.5a). It was somewhat lower and closer to the adjacent wash than Shelter 1. A very large woodrat midden was in the southwest portion of the shelter. Excavators could not determine whether cultural deposits underlay this midden. The main deposition appeared to be in a 3 × 4-m area to the northeast. A layer of cultural fill up to 75 cm in depth extended from the rear of the shelter to well beyond the overhang drip line (Figure 2.6). No structural features or rock alignments were visible prior to subsurface excavation. The cultural deposits were largely unstratified, with the exception of two prominent sterile layers within the fill and several small, ashy lenses in the upper 10 cm (Figure 2.7). These lenses probably represented relatively undisturbed deposits. The presence of rodent burrows and small plastic scraps distributed throughout the fill indicated considerable mixing of the remaining shelter fill.

The most pronounced roof fall layer extended from 5 cm to 27 cm below the surface. Much or all of it appeared to have collapsed during a single event. Cultural fill above and around this fall zone was essentially dry, while that below it was moist, especially in the lower deposits. Except for the ashy lenses, there were no obvious differences between the cultural fill deposited above and that deposited below the fall layer. Individual roof fall rocks were occasionally found within the deposits between the pronounced fall layer and the sterile substrate.

The most distinct and interesting deposit within the shelter was a layer of sterile orange-colored silt lying 40 cm below the surface. This layer averaged approximately 8 cm in thickness and was continuous, although occasionally indistinct, across the central part of the shelter but absent in the southern corner of the excavated deposits. Its distinctive orange color suggested that it had formed and stabilized relatively quickly, without significant mixing with earlier or later deposits. It is likely that this layer represented a single natural deposit, perhaps as a result of a period of extensive flooding in the adjacent wash during which water backed up into the shelter.

Cultural fill within the shelter was a smooth loamy silt with relatively few rocks or pebbles. It was ashy gray-brown in color and contained moderate amounts of flaked stone, burned and unburned bone, and very small pieces of charcoal. Small numbers of ceramic and ground stone artifacts were also present. The last 10 cm of fill below ground surface in the rear of the cave graded gradually upward to sterile brown soil. Other than the few ash lenses described above, the deposits were surprisingly unstratified, presumably due to mixing during and after deposition and to the moist condition of the lower two-thirds of the deposits.

The single architectural feature (Feature 1) was the remains of a 3.0-m-long wall across the center of the shelter and approximately perpendicular to its long axis (Figures 2.5b and 2.6). The wall may have been built as a windbreak, or it may have served to define social space within the shelter. The wall remains varied between 20 cm and 30 cm in height and extended approximately 22 cm below the modern surface. The wall consisted primarily of two courses of horizontally placed conglomerate slabs with an occasional single upright slab. A number of randomly oriented slabs found in the shelter fill adjacent to the wall suggested that the wall might originally have been one or two courses higher. The base of the wall rested on cultural fill deposited some time after the sterile orange silt layer. This would place the construction of this feature during the last half or third of the shelter's occupation (Figure 2.7). The wall did not appear to have been used during the final episodes of shelter occupation, as neither the wall itself nor any wall fall was evident on the modern surface prior to excavation.

Figure 2.5a. AZ T:3:42(ASM), Shelter 2 during excavation, looking northeast.

Figure 2.5b. AZ T:3:42(ASM), Shelter 2 wall (Feature 1), looking south; meter stick in background.

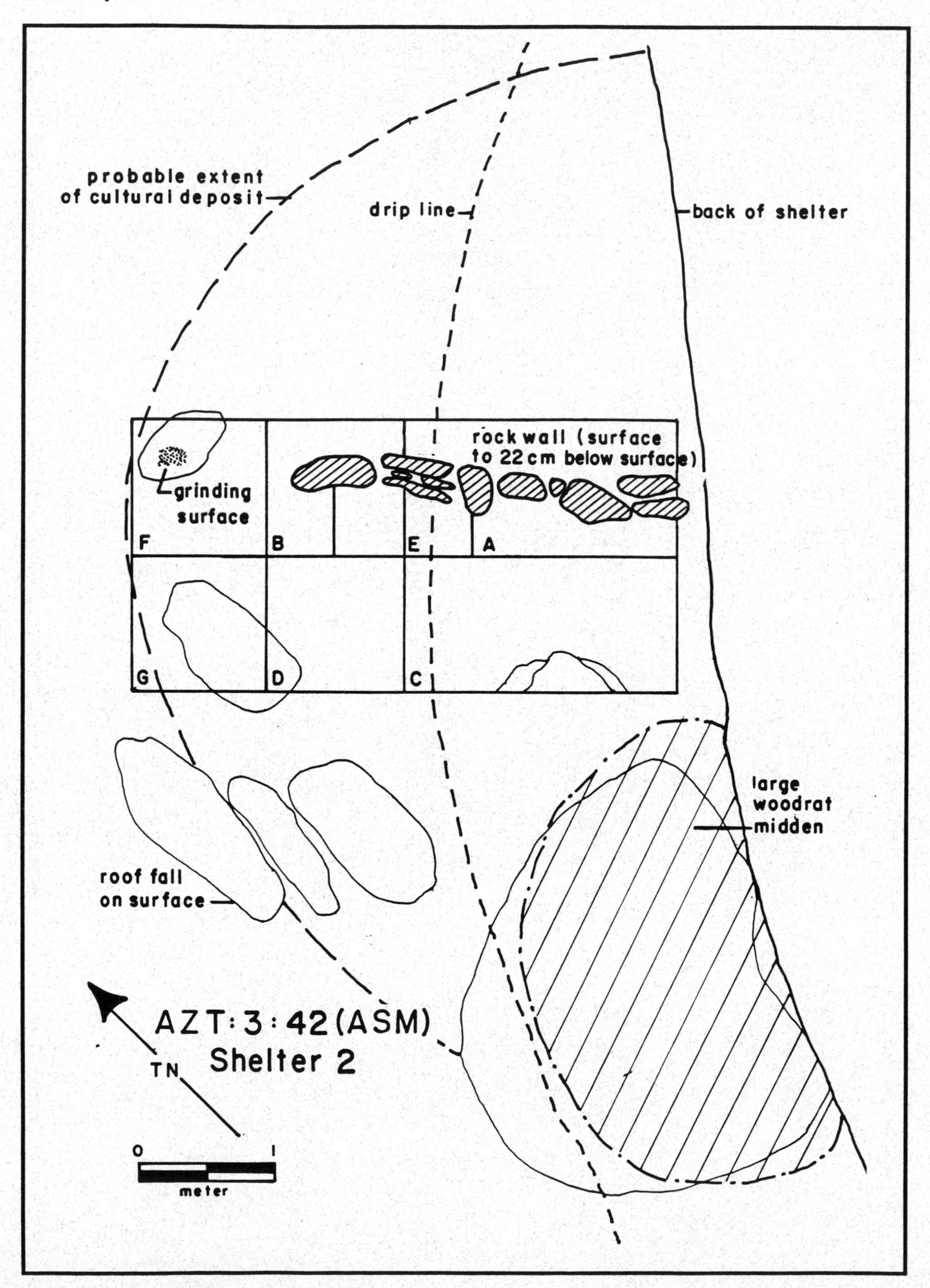

Figure 2.6. AZ T:3:42(ASM), map of Shelter 2.

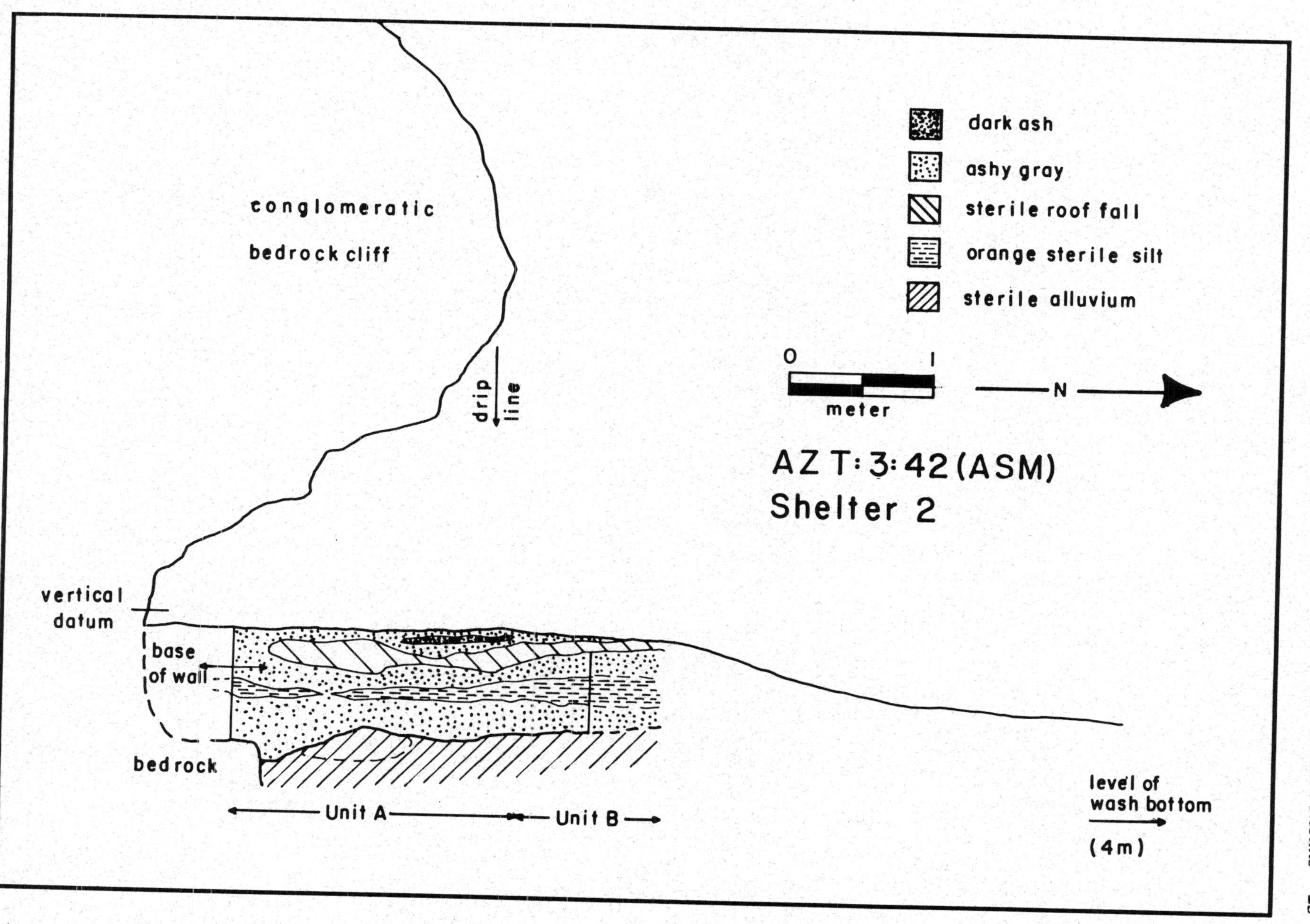

Figure 2.7. AZ T:3:42(ASM), Shelter 2 profile.

AZ T:3:43(ASM)

Site AZ T:3:43(ASM) was in a broad saddle between washes in the valley northwest of Saddleback Mountain at 1800 feet (549 m) above sea level. The substrate consisted of a layer of soft, sandy, light brown soil that varied between 4 cm and 10 cm in thickness. A caliche layer 10 cm thick below the substrate overlay what appeared to be basaltic bedrock. Most of the site was level or very slightly inclined to the southeast, although the eastern corner sloped sharply to the northeast (Figure 2.8). A diffuse artifact scatter distributed evenly across the site covered a 70 × 100-m area on the saddle. This scatter was composed largely of flaked stone, with appreciable amounts of ceramics and ground stone also present. Excavators identified four features at the site, all surface clusters of basalt stones.

The field crews obtained a 25% surface sample by collecting artifacts from one quarter of each 10 × 10-m unit within a gridded area measuring 70 × 80 m. They took some additional judgmental collections at selected locations within and to the east of the gridded area and excavated all features, but Features 1 and 2 most intensively.

Feature 1 was a roughly semicircular ring of stones measuring approximately 2 m in diameter with the opening to the east-northeast. Testing to a depth of 43 cm revealed no subsurface deposits. An irregular pit approximately 50 cm in diameter and 20 cm deep appeared to penetrate the caliche layer within the feature. The pit fill, composed of sterile soil and fist-sized basalt rocks, appeared to be a natural manifestation. Excavators found ceramics, flaked stone, and a grinding slab fragment in close association on and just below the feature surface. The feature probably represented the remains of a shelter, either a windbreak or a foundation for a brush superstructure.

Feature 2 was a roughly T-shaped alignment of large and medium-sized basalt stones measuring 3 × 4 m. Excavators found a few sherds and flaked stone artifacts, including a projectile point, on the surface near this feature. It was not clear whether the stone cluster itself was actually a cultural feature. If so, it might have functioned as a windbreak or shelter foundation. A large boulder used as a grinding stone was 5 m to the northeast of the feature (Figure 2.8). Excavation at Feature 2 extended to a depth of 15 cm.

Feature 3 was a 1.3 × 2.0-m oval rock cluster consisting of a single rock layer 20–30 cm in thickness. Limited testing, to a depth of approximately 10 cm, within the rock oval revealed only sterile soil. The feature appeared to be cultural, although it was not necessarily prehistoric. Its function was problematic; it might have been a collapsed rock pile or cairn or perhaps a post support.

Feature 4 was a 3 × 5-m cluster of medium-sized to large basalt rocks on a moderate slope at the east edge of the site. The rocks were arranged in two or three contiguous circles, each 1.5–2.0 m in size and relatively free of rock within the circles. No artifacts were found in association with the feature, nor was any subsurface cultural evidence revealed during excavation. The feature may well have been cultural and was probably prehistoric; it may have been used for shelter or storage.

AZ T:3:46(ASM)

Site AZ T:3:46(ASM), a small sherd and lithic scatter west of AZ T:3:43(ASM) and north of AZ T:3:42(ASM) (Figure 1.1), was probably the remains of a small activity area. SWCA's field investigators

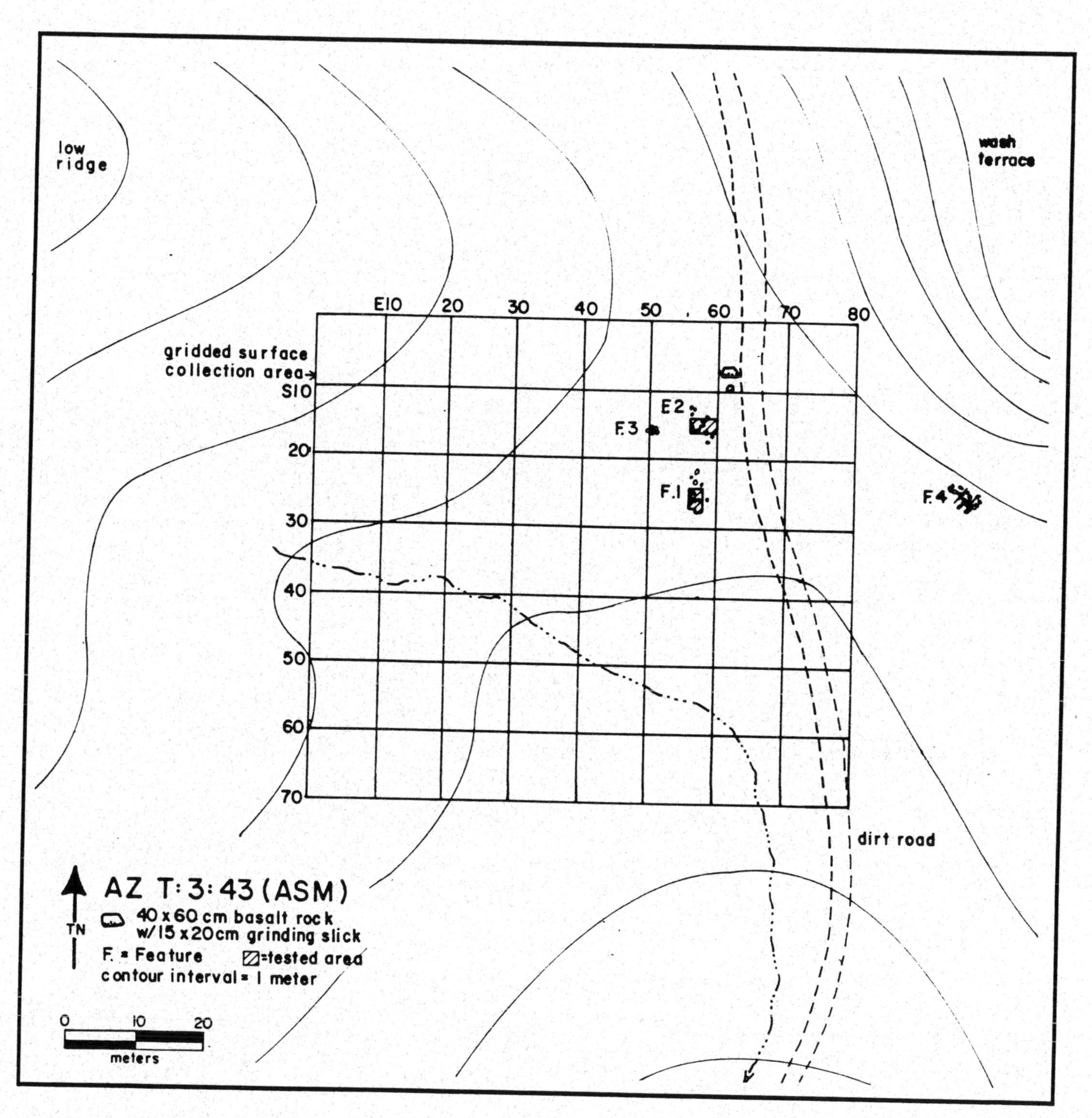

Figure 2.8. AZ T:3:43(ASM), site map.

carried out a modest amount of work at AZ T:3:46(ASM) because they suspected a temporal relationship to Site AZ T:3:43(ASM). The survey team had collected a small ground-slate bird effigy from this site.

The field crews made a 100% surface collection of four 10 × 10-m units centered over the surface feature at the site, a possible cleared area. They trowel-tested within and around the feature, fully defined a small ashy area just south of it, and collected single flotation and radiocarbon samples. A 0.5 × 1.0-m area at the south edge of the activity surface contained ash-stained soil and charcoal to a depth of 10 cm. The stained area contained no fire-cracked rocks and was very disturbed by root growth. It may have been a small fire pit associated with the use of the activity area.

AZ T:3:52(ASM)

Site AZ T:3:52(ASM), dubbed Two Snake Shelter, was at the mouth of a small, narrow valley in the upper Padelford Wash drainage at an elevation of 1900 feet (579 m) (Figure 1.1), approximately two miles southwest of the Windy Well and Saddleback Mountain area sites. The small wash at the north edge of the site was rocky and dry at the time of the site survey and study; however, bedrock catchments in the wash bottom probably hold useful amounts of water at times during the year. The site comprised a rockshelter and an adjacent 20 × 50-m artifact scatter (Figure 2.9). The shelter was quite small, measuring 4.5 m wide × 1.0 m deep × 1.5 m high (Figure 2.10). The artifact scatter contained flaked stone, ground stone, and ceramics, the latter concentrated in front of the shelter. A 2 × 3-m area of ash-stained soil at the west end of the scatter may have indicated the location of a second campsite, although excavation did not reveal cultural deposits.

The field crews made a 100% surface collection of all artifacts within a series of 5 × 5-m grid units. They gridded the rockshelter into six 1 × 1-m units and excavated to a maximum depth of approximately 45 cm, removing approximately 75% of the cultural fill. They also vertically projected the innermost grid corners and inscribed them on the shelter ceiling for future reference. In addition, they tested three other areas with shovel and trowel to depths of approximately 10 cm.

Deposition within the shelter appeared to be primarily colluvial. Excavation revealed a lens of cultural fill that extended from the surface to a depth of 30 cm, grading rapidly downward to a sterile colluvium (Figure 2.10). The cultural fill was gray to gray-brown, ashy to loamy, and relatively free of rocks and pebbles. It contained flaked stone and ground stone artifacts, ceramics, animal bone, macrobotanical material, and ash and charcoal. Although largely unstratified, the cultural fill appeared to have accumulated horizontally over and against the sloping colluvial surface at the back of the shelter. The unstratified nature of the fill was probably due to both relatively low intensity of occupation and subsequent mixing by rodents, insects, and the elements. The cultural fill faded to sterile within 2–3 m of the excavated grid units. It was fairly moist at the time of the original survey in March 1988 but was essentially dry during excavation in late May of the same year.

Ground stone artifacts included two whole grinding slabs, several grinding stone fragments, and a well-shaped one-hand mano. Flaked stone consisted largely of core fragments, shatter, and unmodified interior and exterior flakes, along with a small number of pounders, choppers, and scrapers and a single biface.

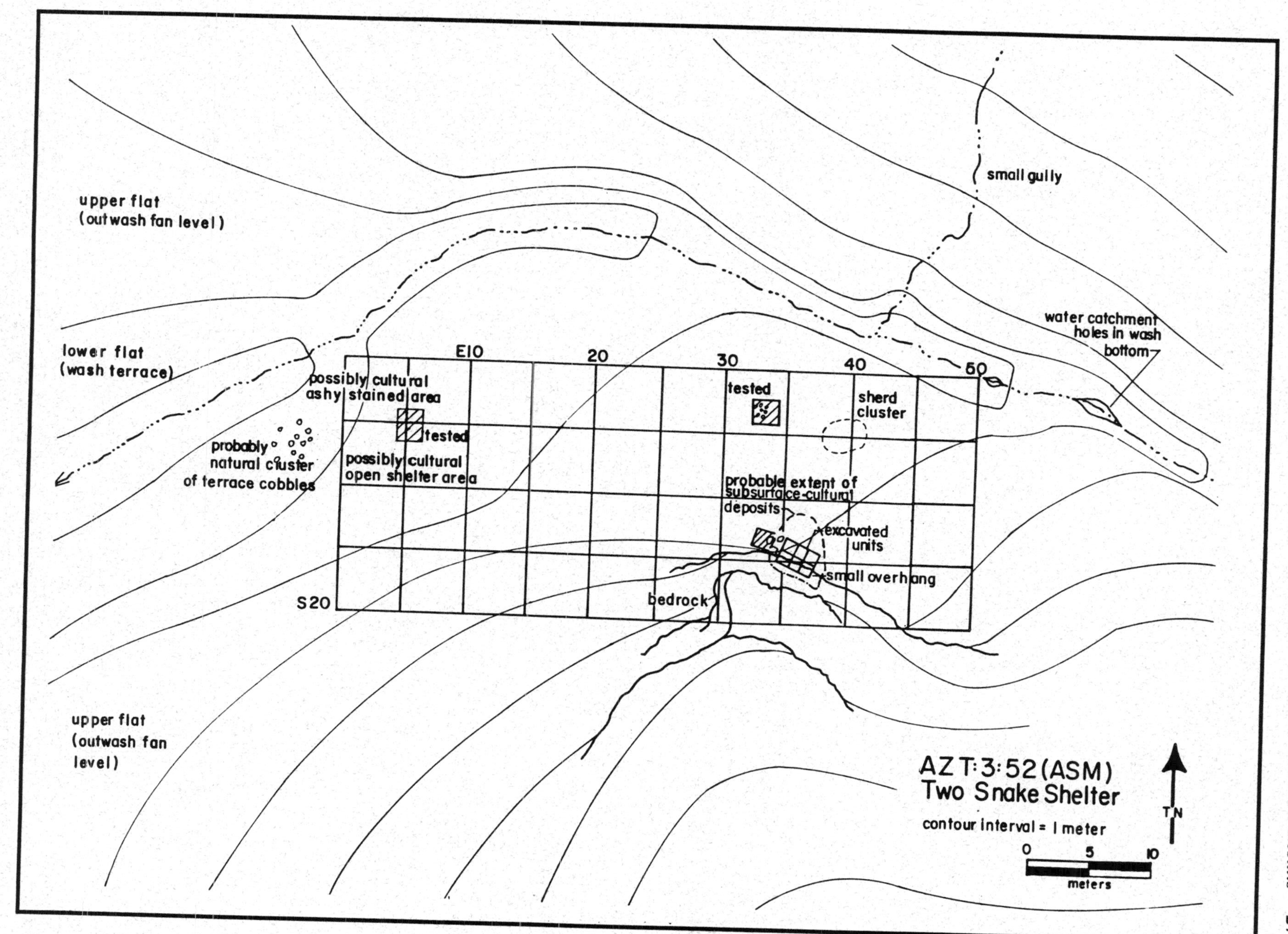

Figure 2.9. AZ T:3:52(ASM), site map.

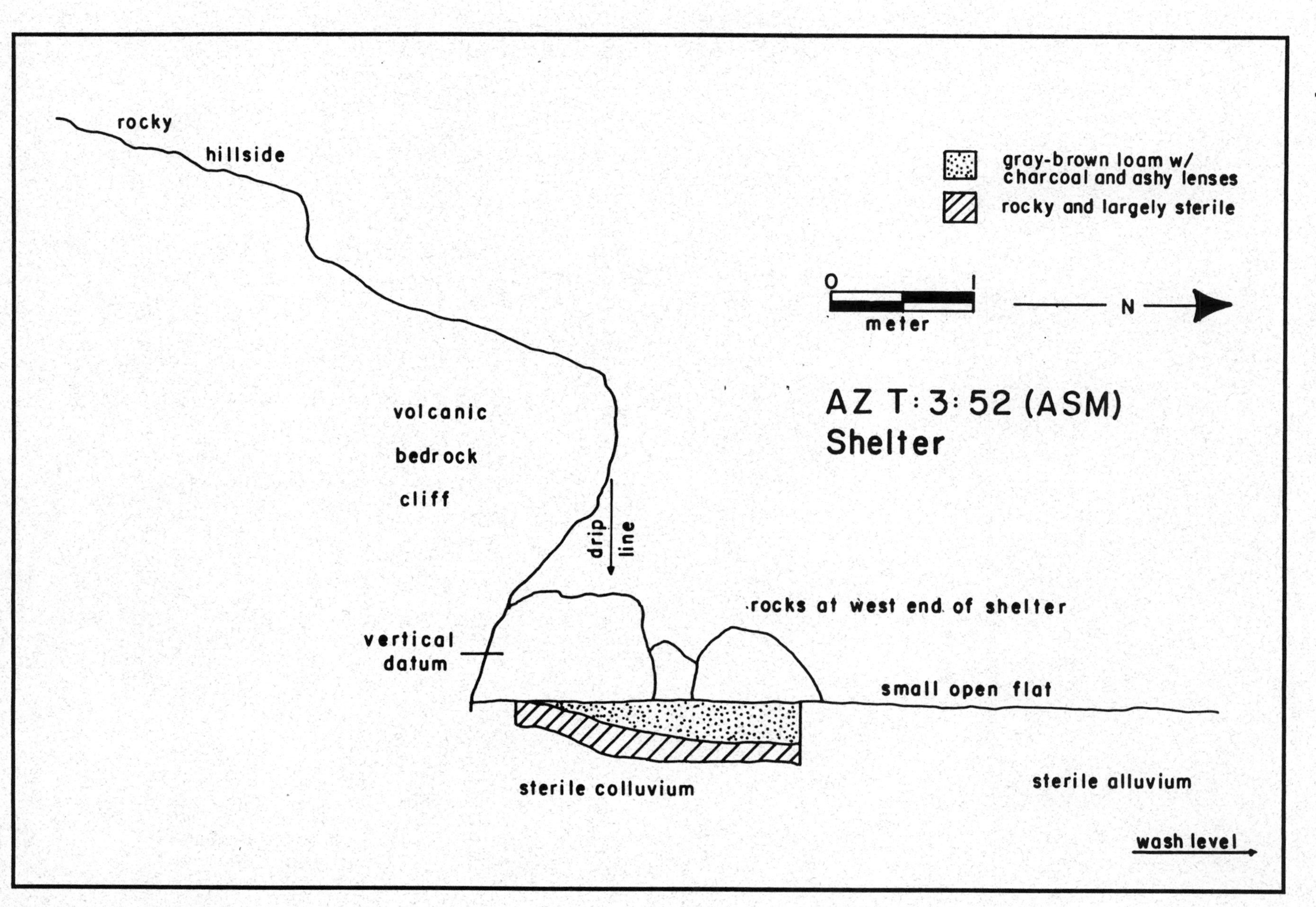

Figure 2.10. AZ T:3:52(ASM), shelter profile.

HISTORIC SITES

AZ T:3:45(ASM)

Site AZ T:3:45(ASM) consisted of three distinct loci (Figure 2.11). Loci A and C were tunnel and shaft features; Locus C included the associated remains of a small encampment. The mining features appeared to be aligned along a single ore vein on the north side of a steep hill near the crest of the Hieroglyphic Mountains. Locus B was a small encampment on a flat a short distance to the north. Investigation of this site included only Loci B and C.

Locus B was on a level bench between two washes to the north of the two mining locations. The remains of the encampment consisted of a 10 × 20–foot outline of stones and a larger (100 × 165–foot) scatter of rusted food cans. The stone cluster appeared to be the remains of a tent base or other structural foundation (Figure 2.12a). The cans consisted primarily of hole-in-cap types with both crimped and soldered seams for evaporated milk, sardines, and other foods. Cans of this type date primarily to the 1920s and earlier (Simonis 1988).

Locus C consisted of a tunnel, a shaft, and a small encampment just above the south bank of a small wash. The tunnel was approximately 100 feet long by 5 feet in diameter, while the adjacent shaft was a little over 30 feet deep. Trash at the small campsite consisted of approximately 15 rusted hole-in-cap crimped-seam cans. A 5-foot diameter circular rock cluster and a water runoff control ditch were also present at this locus, but there were no tailings, the material apparently having been carried away by the wash. Rusted riveted sheet iron in the wash bottom appeared to represent the remains of a small culvert.

The tunnel and shaft followed a narrow ore vein in metamorphic hard rock. The ore itself, like that from other mines in this area, was a dusty yellow-brown in color. No archival information was found for this mine site at the Arizona Department of Mines and Mineral Resources (ADMMR) office or the Bureau of Land Management (BLM) state office. General Land Office (GLO) and Master Title Plat (MTP) records indicate a shaft within lot 9 of this section by December 1941. ADMMR 1997 mining district maps list it as "unknown shaft 9."

The field investigators drew a scale map of the site using measured distances and information from the USGS 7.5 minute topographic map. Surface collections at Loci B and C consisted of representative samples of the various types, forms, and sizes of historic materials present and recording of the number of individual pieces within each type and size class (Chapter 6).

AZ T:3:48(ASM)

This site was on a gently sloping bench between a low hill and an entrenched wash in the Padelford Wash drainage (Figure 2.13). It consisted of a mine shaft and tailings and a nearby encampment marked by a dense trash cluster. The site also included three small prospect holes and a second small trash cluster 500 feet southwest of the main encampment.

The mine was 65 feet long by 13 feet deep by 6.5 feet wide and consisted of two inclines that met under a bridge of rock over the middle 13 feet of the otherwise open pit (Figure 2.13). In the mouth of the north incline was a substantial wooden platform that probably supported a hoist (Figure 2.12b). The

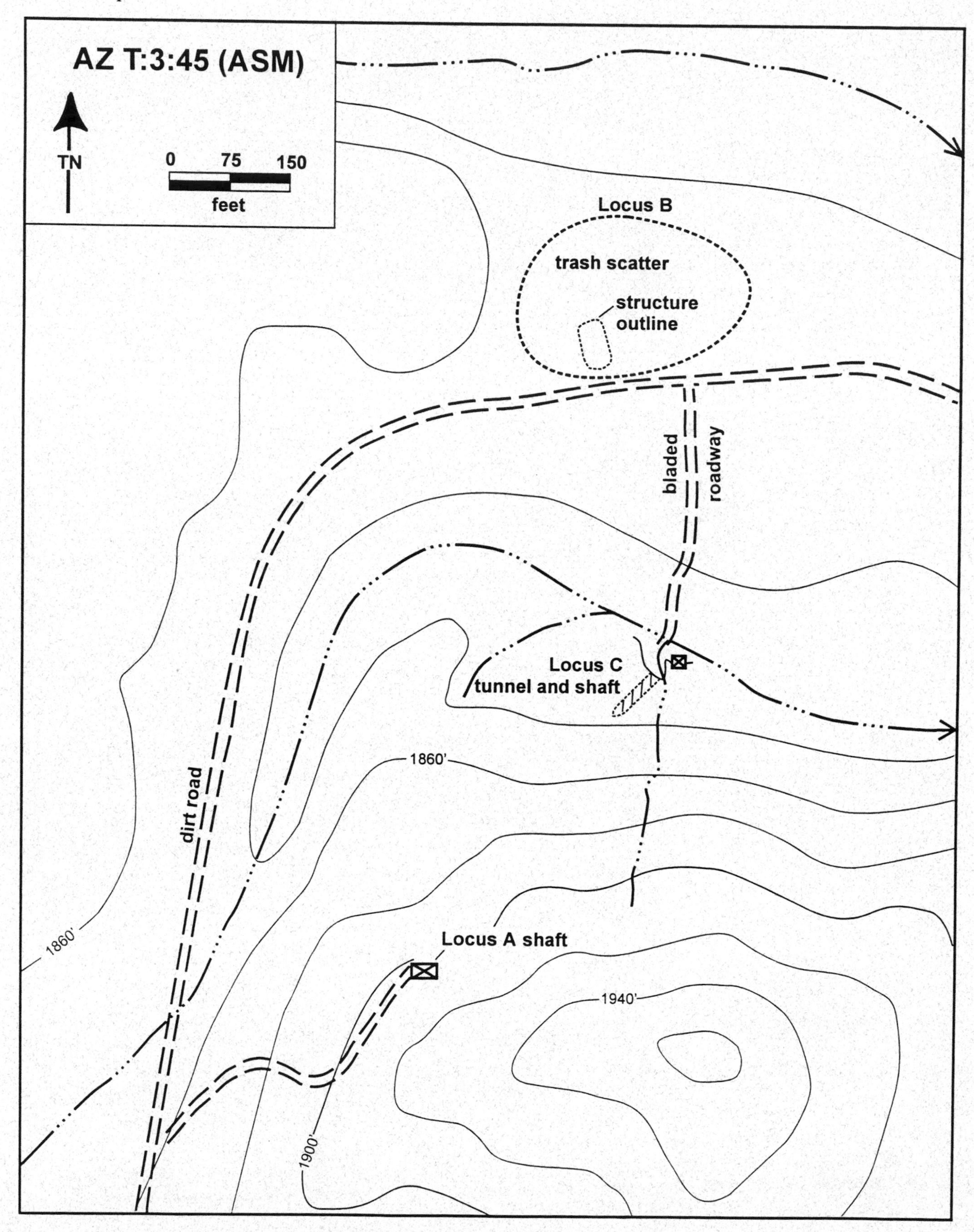

Figure 2.11. AZ T:3:45(ASM), site map.

Figure 2.12a. AZ T:3:45(ASM), Locus B, looking southwest toward structure foundation.

Figure 2.12b. AZ T:3:48 (ASM), head-frame foundation in mouth of north incline shaft.

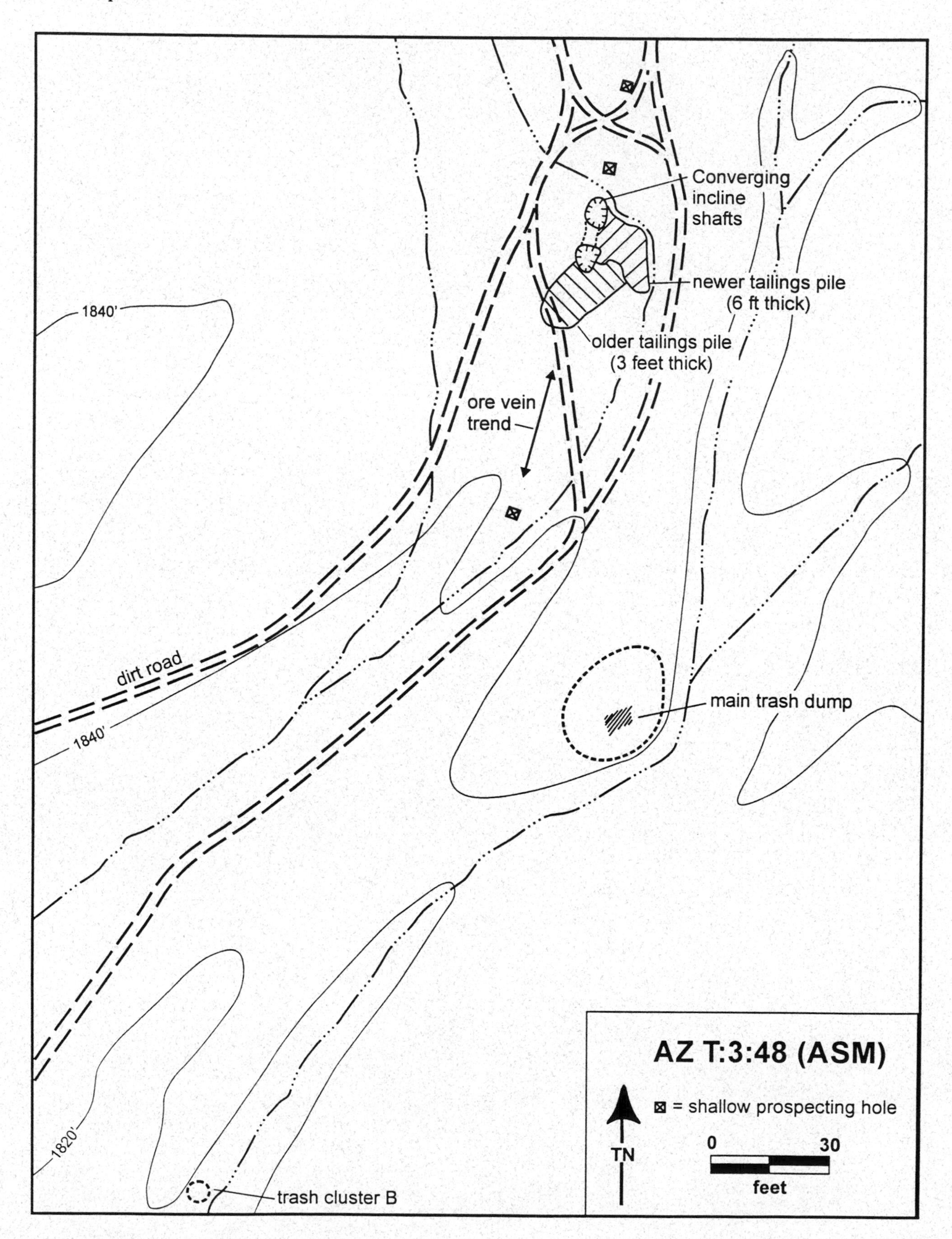

Figure 2.13. AZ T:3:48 (ASM), site map.

south incline appeared to have supported a similar structure. Timbers had collapsed into the north incline, along with small amounts of wire cable. A modern hogwire fence enclosed the mine.

The tailings pile adjacent to the mine had two lobes, the juxtaposition of which indicated that most of the north incline was dug after completion of the one to the south. This conclusion is consistent with the presence of head-frame material in the north incline and its absence in the south incline.

Mineral samples from the mine tailings had a matrix of light colored gray-brown to silver-gray micaceous schist with quartz seams and inclusions. Mineralization occurred in thin seams and surfaces and appeared to be of two types, a blue-green copper mineral and a yellow-brown and rust-red dusty-textured mineral. This ore may have contained both copper and gold. ADMMR 1997 mining district maps show an unknown shaft and prospect at this location, but no other archival information could be found pertaining specifically to this mine there or at the BLM or GLO state offices.

A light scatter of rusted metal artifacts covered the site. The main refuse area, 390 feet to the south of the mine and measuring 100 × 130 feet, was a dense cluster of rusted tin cans, metal fragments, bottle glass, and crockery. The cans were chiefly for milk and food; a few were baking powder and tobacco tins. The site appeared largely undisturbed except for modern dirt roads near the mine and the probable casual removal of some artifacts, especially bottles, by visitors.

The quantity of material in the main trash dump indicated that the occupation was fairly substantial. Although the field crews could not identify the actual living site, it was probably on the flat just north of the trash dump. The smaller dump at the southern site boundary indicated a smaller camp site (Figure 2.13).

The field investigators produced the site map from measured distances and USGS 7.5 minute topographic maps. They collected ore samples from the tailings pile, sorted and counted all of the historic material in the main trash dump (Chapter 6), and collected a representative sample of each type. They also sorted and described artifacts from the smaller trash cluster but did not collect them. Tables of detailed artifact counts appear in Chapter 6.

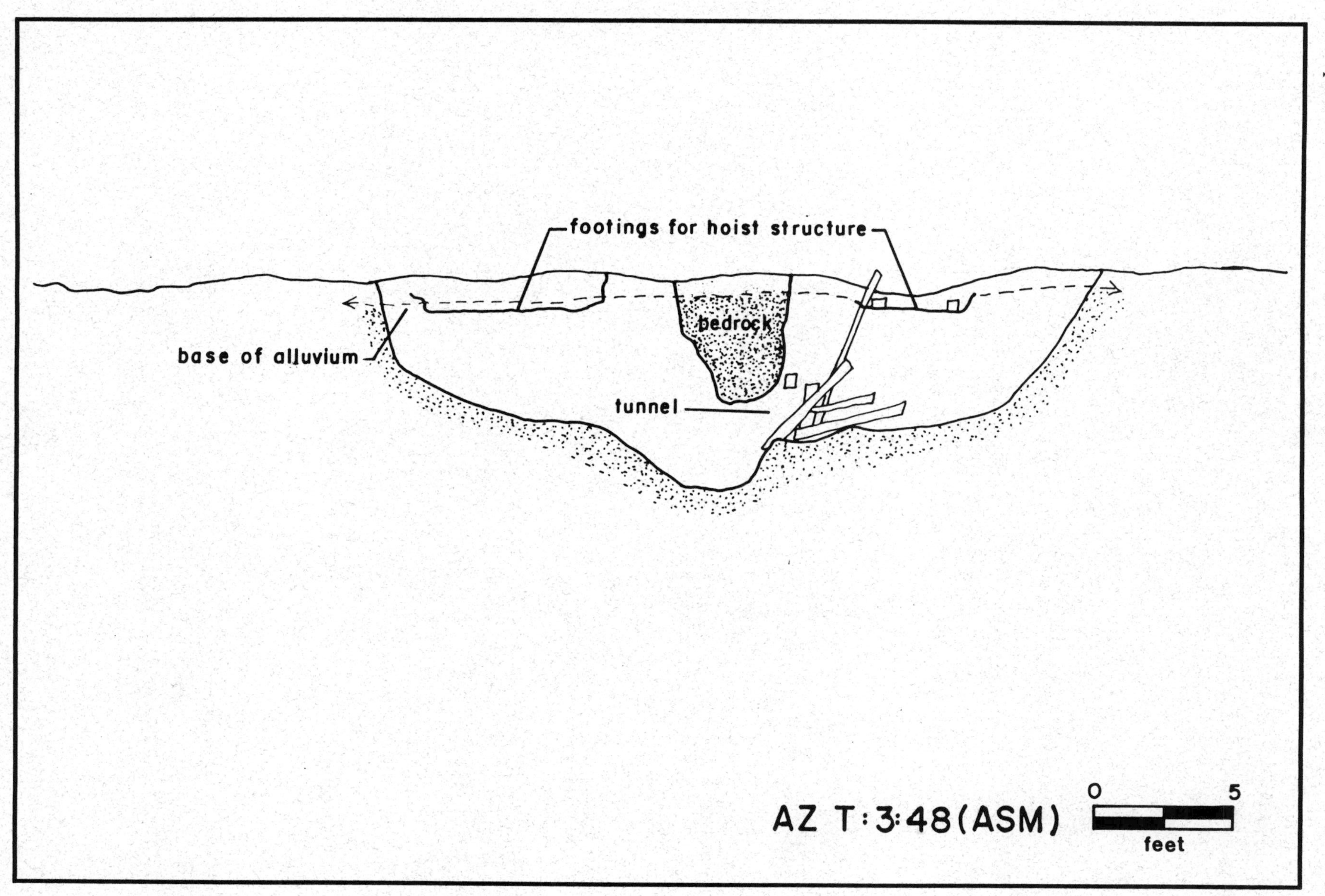

Figure 2.14. AZ T:3:48 (ASM), mine profile.

CHAPTER 3

CERAMIC ANALYSIS

Arthur W. Vokes

SWCA's field investigators recovered a total of 1315 sherds from the five prehistoric sites studied (Table 3.1). Hohokam material was dominant in all of the site collections, but two sites (AZ T:3:42[ASM] and AZ T:3:52[ASM]) also contained sherds assignable to an Upland Yuman, probably Yavapai, cultural tradition. The largest single collection was from AZ T:3:42(ASM), a site with two rockshelters that appeared to have been occupied over an extended period of time. This site assemblage also contained the greatest variety of ceramic types.

CERAMIC TYPES

Plainware

The ceramic assemblages from the excavated sites were dominated by plainwares: Wingfield Plain; Gila Plain, Salt Variety; Gila Plain, Gila Variety; Tizon Wiped; Rimrock Plain (?); and three unnamed types. Of the latter, two are appropriately classified as local variants within the Hohokam tradition, while the third is more closely related to Lower Colorado types.

Wingfield Plain

The most common type recovered (n=599) was Wingfield Plain, which was tempered with phyllite schist. Colton (1941) first described this type, and Weaver (1974) and others (Crown 1981:97-101; Doyel and Elson 1985) have discussed it more recently. Materials in the project collection conformed in all respects to existing descriptions.

Gila Plain, Salt Variety

The excavations yielded 36 sherds of Gila Plain, Salt Variety, a sand-tempered plainware. This was the dominant plainware (47.4%) at AZ T:3:52(ASM) and was also present at AZ T:3:42(ASM) in minor amounts (4.0% of the plainware, 3.6% of the total assemblage). At AZ T:3:52(ASM) this type occurred in all four 10-cm excavation levels in the rockshelter; the sherds recovered represented, at a minimum, two vessels, a bowl and a jar. At AZ T:3:42(ASM), both bowl and jar sherds of Gila Plain, Salt Variety were present in both shelters, probably representing multiple vessels of each form.

Gila Plain, Salt Variety was the dominant plainware recovered from the 1968 excavations at Las Colinas (Crown 1981) and Cashion (Antieau and Pepoy 1981). This type was generally the dominant plainware in Hohokam sites along the Salt River.

Table 3.1. Ceramic Totals, All Sites

Ceramic Type	Site (AZ ...[ASM])					Total
	T:3:41	T:3:42	T:3:43	T:3:46	T:3:52	
Plainware						**961**
Wingfield Plain	283	211	32	70	3	***599***
Gila Plain, Salt Variety		18			18	***36***
Gila Plain, Gila Variety		38	2		1	***41***
Tizon Wiped		175			16	***191***
Rimrock Plain (?)		4				***4***
Type 1	10		5			***15***
Type 2	50			5		***55***
Type 3		1	17			***18***
Unidentified		2				***2***
Hohokam Red Ware						**30**
Wingfield Red	22	2				***24***
Gila Red		2				***2***
Salt Red, Smudged		4				***4***
Decorated Ceramics						**324**
Hohokam Buff Ware						**303**
Casa Grande Red-on-buff		1	3		6	***10***
Late Sacaton/Casa Grande Red-on-buff			13		1	***14***
Sacaton Red-on-buff		2			1	***3***
Santa Cruz Red-on-buff		4				***4***
Unidentified Red-on-buff	3	7	30		10	***50***
Unidentified Hohokam Buff Ware	2	8	180	1	30	***221***
Unidentified Red-on-brown		1				***1***
Other Decorated Wares						**21**
Tonto Polychrome		1				***1***
Jeddito Black-on-yellow		20				***20***
Total	**370**	**501**	**282**	**76**	**86**	**1315**

Gila Plain, Gila Variety

Gila Plain, Gila Variety, recovered from three of the sites investigated, represented only a minor portion (0.7–7.6%) of each assemblage. This type is distinguished by high proportions of micaceous materials in the temper. Although often found in site assemblages throughout the Hohokam region, this variety was much more prevalent in assemblages from sites along the Gila River and probably came into the Agua Fria drainage basin through trade.

Tizon Wiped

Field crews recovered this type from the surface at two sites, AZ T:3:42(ASM) and AZ T:3:52(ASM). In each case, the form and limited distribution of the sherds indicated a single vessel. The material from AZ T:3:42(ASM) was definitely from a jar; the materials from AZ T:3:52(ASM) probably represented a single jar as well, although no rim sherds or other clear evidence of vessel form were present.

The dates of manufacture of Tizon Wiped were probably from the prehistoric until circa A.D. 1900 (Euler and Dobyns 1958). This ware was associated with the historic Havasupai and possibly the Yavapai prior to the 1900s and with prehistoric contexts in central Arizona as early as A.D. 1300 (Pilles 1981).

Rimrock Plain (?)

Four sherds recovered from Shelter 1 at AZ T:3:42(ASM) appeared to represent Rimrock Plain, an Apache plainware of the Verde series that probably postdates the middle of the eighteenth century (Schroeder 1975). The presence of Rimrock Plain would indicate a late occupation or use of the shelter.

Tempering materials in the four sherds included fine subangular clear quartz and considerable amounts of fine mica. The surfaces of the vessel or vessels represented appeared to have been wiped with a coarse material, most noticeably on the interior surfaces. All of the sherds had a dark gray surface color, and the paste was nearly black.

Other Plainware

Also present in the project assemblage were three plainware types that did not conform to any described types. Two of these types appeared to represent local varieties within the Hohokam tradition, while the third was similar to materials recovered from sites in the Tonopah Desert (Vokes 1992).

Type 1

This type is characterized by a coarse paste with a reddish-brown color. The tempering material consists of abundant opaque pieces of quartz and feldspar. Clear quartz particles are also present in smaller quantities; these clear particles tend to be quite rounded and are probably derived from stream sands. The opaque material is generally not as eroded. The size of the particles varies considerably. Tempering material accounts for between a quarter and a third of paste volume. The vessels were fired at a relatively low temperature, resulting in a soft paste that is easily eroded. The sample included sherds from both bowls and jars but in insufficient numbers for definition of the specific forms represented.

Type 2

The second unidentified plainware type appeared to be a hybrid of Type 1 and Wingfield Plain. The paste was essentially the same as in Type 1, although somewhat finer in texture; it would nonetheless be considered a coarse paste. The addition of phyllite particles in the temper distinguishes this type from Type 1. This was the most common of the two possibly local ceramic types, represented by 55 sherds, and was present in two of the site assemblages. In this limited sample, it was associated with Wingfield Plain, Wingfield Red, and Hohokam Buff Ware. The type is most appropriately treated as a local variant of Wingfield Plain.

Both bowl and jar forms were present in the assemblage, but in the majority of cases specific shapes were not identifiable. Two recovered rim sherds appeared to be from hemispherical bowls with direct rims.

Several sherds recovered from AZ T:3:41(ASM) exhibited exterior surface embellishment, which in one instance included irregularities that might have been finger impressions or possibly heavily obliterated coils. A series of thin, rectangular impressions observed on the exterior surface of a jar sherd was not clear enough to discern any patterning because the sherd was small and somewhat eroded. Such embellishments are rare.

Type 3

This type was similar in all respects to a plainware type (Plainware Type A) reported from the Flatiron site and other sites along Fourmile Wash in the Tonopah Desert (Vokes 1992). Characteristics observed in those assemblages suggest relationships with the Lower Colorado River ceramic tradition. In both these examples and the Hieroglyphic Mountains assemblage, the type characteristics were a coarse reddish-brown paste and temper consisting predominantly of rounded to subangular particles of clear quartz and feldspar (Vokes 1992). In the Fourmile Wash assemblages the type was dominant; in the Hieroglyphic Mountains assemblage, it was a minor component represented by only 18 sherds. Seventeen of the sherds came from one site (AZ T:3:43[ASM]) and probably represented a single vessel.

Hohokam Red Ware

Two sites (AZ T:3:41[ASM] and AZ T:3:42[ASM]) yielded 30 red-slipped sherds. Eighty percent were Wingfield Red; the remainder were either Salt Red or Gila Red.

Wingfield Red

As its name implies, this type is a slipped variety of Wingfield Plain. The slip is relatively thin, with a reddish to reddish-brown color. Wingfield Red sherds (n=24) accounted for just under 4% of the sherds of the Wingfield tradition recovered from all sites in the project area. The type accounted for 6% of the total assemblage from AZ T:3:41(ASM), and a mere 0.4% of the sample from AZ T:3:42(ASM). The Wingfield Red sherds from AZ T:3:41(ASM) were in a concentration that contained both jar and bowl forms, indicating at least two vessels.

The temporal associations of Wingfield Red are as yet poorly understood. This ware first appeared in the Sedentary period, and its production continued into the late Classic period. In the 1968 excavations at Las Colinas (Crown 1981), Wingfield Red was the dominant redware in the Late Sedentary and Early Classic period material recovered; its pre-eminence at the site was lost to Gila Red following the Soho phase, but it was present until the final occupation.

Gila Red

The two Gila Red sherds recovered from Level 3 of Shelter 1 at AZ T:3:42(ASM) were probably from the same vessel, a bowl that had been slipped inside and out. The slip contained a considerable quantity of fine mica.

Salt Red

Four Salt Red sherds came from Shelter 2 at AZ T:3:42(ASM). They were all from bowls with smudged interiors and could have originated from the same vessel. One sherd was considerably thicker than the others, however, and may have represented a second vessel.

Decorated Ceramics

Hohokam Buff Ware

The majority (77.8%) of the decorated ceramics recovered were Hohokam Buff Ware, with sherds representing late forms of Sacaton Red-on-buff or Casa Grande Red-on-buff (n=27) dominating the identifiable types. The bulk of the Hohokam material consisted of either undecorated fragments of buffware or red-on-buff sherds that could not be confidently identified to type.

Material from one of the shelters at AZ T:3:42(ASM) included Colonial period sherds, all of them from a flared bowl form with the "flying bird" motif and trailing lines on the exterior surface, and it is quite possible that they represented a single vessel. The Sacaton phase material, also from this site, came from both shelters. The late Sacaton or early Classic period material was from a Gila-shouldered vessel and was unusual in that the surface was polished. The design consisted of a sectioned pattern of rectilinear elements.

The decorated material from AZ T:3:43(ASM) was transitional between Sedentary period styles and those found in the Classic period. The material was probably derived from a single vessel that exhibited elements attributable to both complexes. The vessel was a jar with a modified Gila shoulder and a vertical neck. The decorated zones were separated by encircling scalloped lines at the neck and along the shoulder. A similar layout appeared in material from the shelter at AZ T:3:52(ASM).

A number of contexts at both AZ T:3:42 and AZ T:3:52(ASM) yielded Classic period ceramics. The material from AZ T:3:42(ASM) was from a single jar with a high, cylindrical neck.

Tonto Polychrome

The one Tonto Polychrome sherd recovered, a large segment from the rim of a recurved Tonto Polychrome bowl, came from Shelter 1 at AZ T:3:42(ASM). Both the interior and exterior surfaces were decorated. The interior surface decoration was in the Gila style, while the exterior design incorporated red pigment into the design field, the hallmark of Tonto Polychrome. Archaeologists believe Tonto Polychrome to be derived from Gila Polychrome; it appears in the archaeological record at about A.D. 1350 and occurs into the Protohistoric period. Crown and Sires (1984) and Sires (1984) have identified both Gila and Tonto polychrome as diagnostic for the Polvorón phase of the post-Classic period in the Hohokam chronology. Jeddito Black-on-yellow and Classic period Hohokam Red Wares, such as Salt Red, are at least partially contemporaneous with Tonto Polychrome.

Jeddito Black-on-yellow

The twenty sherds of Jeddito Black-on-yellow recovered from various excavation levels within Shelter 1 at AZ T:3:42(ASM) appeared to be from one bowl. This type has a temporal span (A.D. 1300-1400) roughly equivalent to that of Tonto Polychrome and a wide geographic distribution. The locus of manufacture for Jeddito Black-on-yellow was the general region of the Hopi Mesas, north of the Little Colorado River. These sherds probably represent Hopi trade to the Yavapai.

SITE ASSEMBLAGES

AZ T:3:41(ASM)

Plainwares (92.7%) dominated the assemblage from AZ T:3:41(ASM), with Wingfield Plain occurring most frequently. However, the frequency (17.6%) of local varieties in the collection was unusually high. Multiple vessels of these local varieties clearly were represented, as sherds from both bowls and jars were present. In addition, one rim sherd appeared to represent a scoop. The greatest concentration of this material was from the central portion of the site near Feature 1.

Wingfield Plain sherds occurred throughout the site, with noticeable concentrations in the areas surrounding both of the surface features. In contrast, the greatest concentration of Wingfield Red was around Feature 2. Surface proveniences in this area produced nearly 70% of the redware sherds. Apparently two concentrations represented two discrete deposits, with sherds from a bowl in one area and sherds from a jar in the other. The remaining Wingfield Red material was largely from the area of Feature 1. The material here was not as concentrated and was from at least two vessels, a bowl and a jar.

All buffware sherds were from the eastern portion of the site. Although analysts could not assign the sherds to specific types, they made some observations. The quality of the paint and the heaviness of its application suggested that the material predated Classic period Casa Grande Red-on-buff. This type tends not to have large areas of solid color, and the pigment is often a thinner, "lifeless" red (Haury 1945:53). The pigment on the material from AZ T:3:41(ASM) was heavy and a dark red-brown color.

The ceramic evidence suggested that this site might represent a Sedentary or early Classic period occupation. Although the decorated sherds could not be used to demonstrate this directly, Sedentary period material is more likely. The presence of a relatively high number of Wingfield Red sherds, a type that is known from Sedentary and Classic period contexts elsewhere (Crown 1981), provides indirect evidence for this temporal assignment.

AZ T:3:42(ASM)

Site AZ T:3:42(ASM) produced the most diverse ceramic assemblage of the sites investigated during this project. Including the material from the two rockshelters and the exterior artifact scatter, this site represented a temporal span from the late Colonial period to the end of the prehistoric era, possibly into the Historic period.

The deposits in both shelters appeared to have been subjected to substantial bioturbation, as fragments of the same vessel were recovered from multiple excavation levels (Tables 3.2 and 3.3). This was especially true for Shelter 1, which contained sherds from one Jeddito Black-on-yellow bowl in all levels. Therefore, little insight could be gained from reviewing the stratigraphic sequence of these units. However, the two shelters exhibited significant differences.

The earliest material, consisting of four sherds of Santa Cruz Red-on-buff, possibly from the same vessel, came from the lowest 20 cm of the fill in Shelter 2. Other decorated sherds were present but were too eroded or too small to permit identification. Among this material was an unidentified red-on-brown sherd. Investigators have recovered red-on-brown ceramics of apparently local origin that exhibited painted designs identical to those on Colonial period red-on-buff types at Las Colinas (Abbott 1988) and Cashion (Antieau and Pepoy 1981) in the Phoenix basin and at the Beardsley Canal Site (Weed 1972) in the Agua Fria drainage.

The upper 40 cm of fill in Shelter 2 appeared to have suffered more bioturbation than the lower portions of the deposit. All four upper levels contained sherds from a Salt Red, Smudged bowl and late Sacaton and Casa Grande red-on-buff sherds as well.

On the basis of stratigraphic position only, evidence for the earliest use of Shelter 1 was a Sacaton Red-on-buff sherd recovered from Level 4. As noted above, however, vertical position of cultural material may be of little significance. The presence of Jeddito Black-on-yellow and Tonto Polychrome sherds indicated that the shelter was used late in the prehistoric sequence. The presence of Tizon Wiped sherds on the surface outside the shelters also indicated a late prehistoric, protohistoric, or historic occupation or use of the site by Yavapai groups.

The paucity of Wingfield Red in the assemblage is intriguing. Analysts should not rely too heavily on negative data and must always take into account sampling error in the interpretation of small assemblages such as this one. It is possible, however, that the low frequency of Wingfield Red reflects a decline in activity at the site during the late Sedentary and early Classic periods, when Wingfield Red was most

Table 3.2. Stratigraphic Distribution of Ceramic Types in Shelter 1, Site AZ T:3:42(ASM)

Ceramic Type	**Stratigraphic Level***					
	0–10	10–20	20–30	30–40	40–50	50–60
Plainware						
Wingfield Plain	26	32	26	36	18	12
Gila Plain, Salt Variety	1	2	2	3	1	
Gila Plain, Gila Variety	2	4	13	7		8
Tizon Wiped						
Rimrock Plain (?)	1	1		2		
Type 1						
Type 2						
Type 3	1					
Unidentified	2					
Hohokam Red Ware						
Wingfield Red		1				
Gila Red						
Salt Red, Smudged			2			
Decorated Ceramics						
Hohokam Buff Ware						
Casa Grande Red-on-buff						
Late Sacaton/Casa Grande Red-on-buff						
Sacaton Red-on-buff				1		
Santa Cruz Red-on-buff						
Unidentified Red-on-buff			1	1		1
Unidentified Hohokam Buff Ware	1	3	2	1		
Unidentified Red-on-brown						
Other Decorated Wares						
Tonto Polychrome			1			
Jeddito Black-on-yellow	5	3	6	5		1
Total	**39**	**46**	**53**	**56**	**19**	**22**

*cm below surface

Table 3.3. Stratigraphic Distribution of Ceramic Types in Shelter 2, Site AZ T:3:42(ASM)

Ceramic Type	**Stratigraphic Level***						
	0–10	10–20	20–30	30–40	40–50	50–60	60–70
Plainware							
Wingfield Plain	6		6	15		15	
Gila Plain, Salt Variety		1	1	4	1		2
Gila Plain, Gila Variety		1	1		2		
Tizon Wiped							
Rimrock Plain (?)							
Type 1							
Type 2							
Type 3							
Unidentified							
Hohokam Red Ware							
Wingfield Red							
Gila Red							
Salt Red, Smudged	1	1	1	1			
Decorated Ceramics							
Hohokam Buff Ware							
Casa Grande Red-on-buff				1			
Late Sacaton/Casa Grande Red-on-buff							
Sacaton Red-on-buff		1					
Santa Cruz Red-on-buff					2	2	
Unidentified Red-on-buff				1	1		
Unidentified Hohokam Buff Ware				1	1		
Unidentified Red-on-brown					1		
Other Decorated Ceramics							
Tonto Polychrome							
Jeddito Black-on-yellow							
Total	**7**	**4**	**9**	**23**	**8**	**17**	**2**

*cm below surface

prevalent (Crown 1981). The low frequency of Sacaton Red-on-buff is consonant with this interpretation as well. Use of the site may then have increased again during or after the late Classic period.

AZ T:3:43(ASM)

The ceramic evidence indicated that this site was occupied for a relatively short period during the transition between the Sedentary and Classic periods. The assemblage was dominated by Hohokam Buff Ware types, which made up 80% of the collection. This figure may be somewhat misleading, however, because all of the buffware sherds were associated with Feature 1 and probably represented a single, moderately large jar with attributes of both Casa Grande and Sacaton red-on-buff. One of the sherds was from a vertical neck but was not complete enough for measurement of the neck's height. Most of the body was missing; what remained was badly eroded. The vessel had a modified Gila shoulder with an encircling undulating line, and a convoluted line encircled the base of the neck. The remaining ceramic material was lightly dispersed across the surface of the site.

AZ T:3:46(ASM)

This assemblage appeared to reflect a short-term occupation. The dominant type was Wingfield Plain, accounting for over 92% of the ceramic material. As with AZ T:3:41(ASM), this site contained plainware of probable local origin (Type 2). Only a single sherd of coarse Hohokam Buff Ware was present. The preponderance of Wingfield Plain and the presence of a buffware sherd indicated a Hohokam-affiliated population.

AZ T:3:52(ASM)

The assemblage from this site represented at least two distinct occupations, one by prehistoric Hohokam populations and one by the Yavapai. The Hohokam occupation had centered on the small rockshelter that was the principal feature at the site. The ceramics, specifically the Sacaton Red-on-buff sherds in the shelter fill, indicated initial occupation during the Sedentary period, perhaps in the late Sedentary. Other sherds appeared to be from a single large Casa Grande Red-on-buff jar. This material was recovered from all levels in the shelter, indicating extensive bioturbation of the deposit. The Sacaton and Casa Grande material may have been deposited during the same period of occupation. Evidence reported from the 1982-1983 excavations at Las Colinas (Abbott 1988) indicated that these types co-occurred at sites in the Salt River basin.

The dominance of Gila Plain, Salt Variety suggested a more direct affiliation between the population that occupied the shelter and that of the Salt River basin, where this plainware is much more commonly recovered. However, the small number of sherds in the project assemblage lends itself to sampling error, and the hypothesis must be regarded as speculative.

A concentration of Tizon Wiped sherds on the surface outside of the shelter indicated a second, later occupation. This ceramic type, part of the Tizon Brown Ware tradition, is associated with upland Yuman populations (Euler and Dobyns 1958). The most likely group is the Yavapai, whose territory in historic times included the region north of the Gila River (Pilles 1981).

SUMMARY

The ceramic evidence suggested that the Hohokam first occupied or used the project area during the middle to late Colonial period and continued to exploit the region following the Classic period, possibly into the Historic period. Initial occupation appears to have been by populations with ties to the northern portion of the Hohokam region, specifically the area of the Agua Fria River and its tributaries, where the dominant ware was Wingfield Plain. This time period witnessed a general expansion of Hohokam influence throughout much of the desert region of Arizona (Cordell 1984). The evidence suggested that the occupation of the project area was of a limited and perhaps intermittent nature and was never intensive.

Historic sources indicate that sometime following the decline of the Hohokam tradition, the Yavapai, an upland Yuman group, occupied the region north of the Gila and Salt rivers. Evidence of their use of the project area came from two sites, AZ T:3:42(ASM) and AZ T:3:52(ASM). Both sites had concentrations of Tizon Wiped, a distinctive brownware associated with the Pai and Yavapai cultural tradition, and in both cases the concentrations were on the open surface outside the rockshelters.

CHAPTER 4

FLAKED STONE ANALYSIS

Donald R. Keller

GOALS AND METHODS

The analysis of prehistoric flaked stone artifacts included all 1122 pieces of flaked stone collected from Sites AZ T:3:41(ASM), AZ T:3:42(ASM), AZ T:3:43(ASM), and AZ T:3:52(ASM) and an additional 35 items from AZ T:3:46(ASM), a locus closely associated with AZ T:3:42(ASM) and AZ T:3:43(ASM). The purpose of the analysis was to record quantitative information concerning three primary attributes: form (including detail retouch), use wear, and raw material type. Analysis of form included differentiating between cores and flakes and considering the kind and position of detail on unifacial or bifacial retouch. Use wear analysis determined the type of wear and its location on the artifact.

Most of the analysis was by naked eye, with examination of some use-wear evidence by low-power (10–30X) binocular microscope. Although the typology employed in the analysis involved both form and function, definitions of particular artifact types were morphological. Labels implying function are for descriptive economy, to convey the most general names and assumed functions associated with these forms.

Typology

To classify project flaked stone, the analyst used standard criteria that are compatible with the discussions and definitions of Bordaz (1970), Bordes (1969), Crabtree (1972), and Keller (1984). Initially the analyst sorted the flakes by size in increments of 1 cm, 2 cm, and 7 cm and differentiated between exterior and interior flakes based on an estimate of the amount of cortex remaining on the dorsal surface of a given flake. Exterior flakes were those exhibiting more than one-third cortex and interior flakes those exhibiting less than one-third. Shatter included core and flake fragments that lacked diagnostic features.

Pounding stones were generally cores or unmodified rocks that bore percussion wear and blunting on edges or surfaces forming relatively obtuse (greater than 90°) angles. Choppers showed generalized blunting on edges with relatively acute (smaller than 60°) angles. Scrapers were well-shaped unifacially retouched pieces made on flakes, scraper planes were large scrapers made on cores, and flake scrapers were less formally retouched pieces. Thin biface knives and thinning and resharpening flakes were products of well-controlled soft-hammer percussion, with resharpening flakes showing actual use wear on a detached edge segment. Flake knives had less extensive bifacial flaking of various kinds along one or more flake edges. Thick bifaces were generally ovoid forms with hard-hammer or soft-hammer percussion flaking over most or all surfaces. Drills were bifacially flaked pieces with relatively narrow tips and generally beveled, trapezoidal cross-sections. Rubbing stones were small, generally unmodified pieces with one or more smoothed surfaces.

Laboratory personnel assigned utilization evidence to one of five functional classes on the basis of use wear form, assuming only a very general level of functional inference. Wear evidence took the form of unifacial microflaking and smoothing (scraping), bifacial microflaking and edge smoothing (cutting), heavier random flaking and blunting on moderately angled edges (chopping), and heavy blunting on wide-angled edges and surfaces (pounding). Rubbing evidence took the form of faceting or smoothing of surfaces or steep-angled edges, caused by abrasive wear.

Material Types

The prehistoric occupants of the project area used a considerable variety of igneous and metamorphic rock types. Chert was present in the assemblage in a variety of colors, including red and yellow types generally called jasper, and chalcedony, distinguished from other cherts by its translucence and finely textured surface. Other metamorphics included schist and quartzite. The quartz collected during the project was almost entirely of the vein variety and was opaque white with few apparent crystal surfaces. The assemblage also included a few pieces of blackish-colored vein quartz and one piece of fully transparent crystal quartz. The rhyolite in the collection was a reddish tan variety with relatively few large phenocrysts and good knapping qualities. The obsidian present consisted of good-quality black-colored varieties. Other igneous materials included a considerable variety of large-grained materials such as basalt, granite, gabbro, and tufa. Fine-grained brown and black igneous materials resembling andesite or dark lustrous rhyolite also were present; the latter also has good knapping qualities.

INTERPRETATION

The analyst expected that the flaked stone analysis would provide not just a basic description of project materials, but a functional perspective on the nature of and changes in prehistoric and protohistoric activities at individual sites and in the project area as a whole. This information can form a basis for intersite and regional comparisons of quantified data, which may be especially useful in documenting specific subsistence activities in conjunction with ethnographic studies of the Yavapai. Tables 4.1 through 4.8, at the end of the chapter, summarize the analysis results.

Use Wear

Use wear appeared on 17.9% of the total project collection, with frequencies for individual site assemblages ranging between 9.1% and 25.0%. These figures were within the range expected for camp and subsistence sites and contrasted with the frequencies of 3% to 7% that have been observed at lithic procurement and workshop sites (Keller 1984). The notably low frequency of 9.1% recorded in Shelter 2 at AZ T:3:42 (ASM) was due primarily to the very small amount of scraping wear in that assemblage.

In general, pounding and scraping wear dominated in the project assemblage. The level of chopping use wear was moderate, with lesser levels of cutting and rubbing use wear. Exceptions to these general patterns included the very low frequencies for scraping wear from Shelter 2 at AZ T:3:42(ASM) (noted above), a relatively high frequency of cutting wear from AZ T:3:43(ASM), and little evidence of chopping wear from AZ T:3:52(ASM). Given the limited and varying sizes of the individual site and locus collections, much of the observed variation within the overall pattern may be attributable to idiosyncratic behavior prehistorically and to vagaries in subsequent deposition and collection recovery.

Form

Shatter, interior flakes, core fragments, and exterior flakes dominated the flaked stone assemblage, with a much smaller number of cores (Table 4.1). Retouched pieces and other tools were fewer in number. Figure 4.1 illustrates a sample of these items. The most common tool types were fist-sized pounding stones and small flake scrapers. Choppers, scrapers, and bifaces were moderate in number, especially thin knife-type bifaces produced by soft-hammer percussion.

Each of the individual sites and site loci reflected this general pattern, with the following exceptions: Shelter 2 at AZ T:3:42(ASM) appeared to be deficient in the whole core, pounding stone, scraper, and flake scraper categories; at AZ T:3:43(ASM) shatter and whole core forms were under-represented, while interior flakes were in relative abundance; and unmodified interior flakes were nearly absent at nearby AZ T:3:46(ASM).

As noted above, the tool types found in Shelter 2 at AZ T:3:42(ASM) were consistent with the use-wear patterns observed for this same locus, supporting the premise of a functional difference between Shelter 2 and the other site loci. Both Shelter 1 at AZ T:3:42(ASM) and the open flat west of the shelters contained a relative abundance of pounding stones, choppers, and flake scrapers. The artifacts from these proveniences appeared to be much more functionally similar to one another than to those from Shelter 2.

Interpretations involving relatively large artifacts such as pounding stones should be made with care. These artifacts, like ground stone, no doubt undergo considerable reuse and are probably found in disproportionate numbers in the last part of a site to be used. Of related interest was the observation that the larger artifacts tended to be found on the surface and uppermost layers of excavation units at Sites AZ T:3:42(ASM) and AZ T:3:52(ASM), whereas smaller artifacts were more evenly distributed throughout the fill. This pattern may be due both to greater reuse of larger pieces and to purely mechanical processes of fill formation.

Material

The raw material most frequently present as core, core fragment and shatter, and pounding stones and choppers was quartz, as shown in Table 4.1. In contrast, unmodified exterior and interior flakes included a more evenly balanced range of materials. In fact, the flake tool categories, overall, exhibited little use of quartz. This evidence, and the amount and kind of use evidence seen on the core forms and shatter, strongly indicated that the inhabitants of the studied sites had carried out relatively little core reduction in producing tools. Rather, the abundance of core forms and shatter reflected relatively heavy pounding and chopping tool use.

Unaccounted for in the project collection were the bases against which the observed pounding and chopping tools may have been used. Some portion of the 19 pieces of grinding slabs or metates recorded by the project (Chapter 5) may have served this purpose. The site occupants may have used numerous bedrock or large-boulder pounding locations, although only the two locations shown on the AZ T:3:42(ASM) and AZ T:3:43(ASM) site maps (Figures 2.4 and 2.10) exhibited clear enough wear to show such use, and this wear was primarily from grinding rather than pounding. Russell (1908) reported that the Pima used wooden mortars with stone pounding tools; however, much of the pounding wear seen in the present collection appeared to represent impacts of stone against stone.

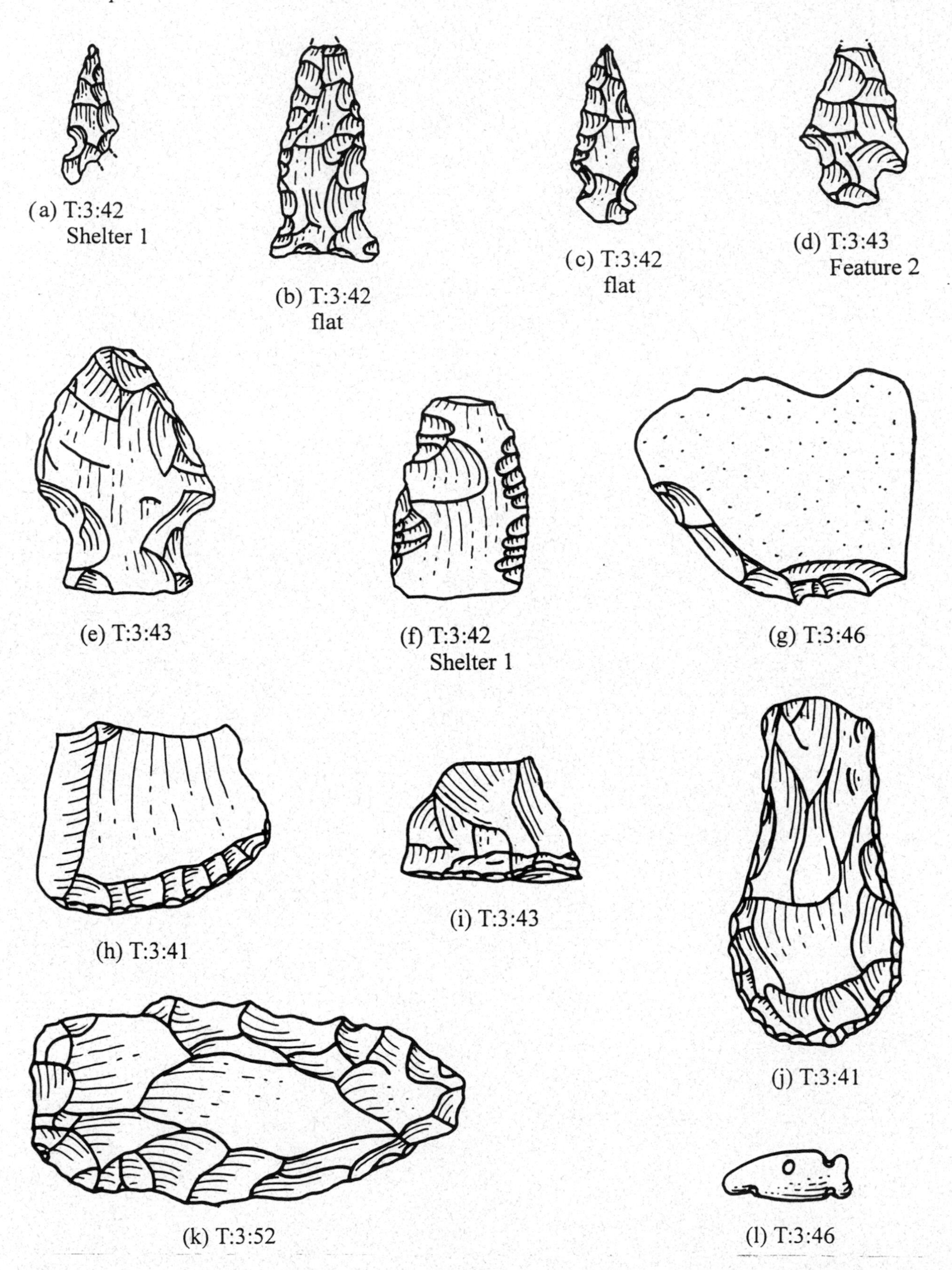

Figure 4.1. Selected lithic artifacts: (a) Desert Side-notched projectile point; (b-d) projectile points; (e) hafted knife; (f) flake knife; (g-k) unifacial scrapers; (l) ground-slate bird pendant. All artifacts actual size. Site numbers are ASM designations (AZ...[ASM]).

Material Sources

Sources for the raw material in the flaked stone assemblage appeared to be variable. The chert, chalcedony, and obsidian were probably exotic. Chert and chalcedony may have been available as stream gravels within the Agua Fria, Verde, and Salt River drainages. Potential sources for obsidian include the Government Mountain and Partridge Creek areas in northern Arizona and the Burro Creek, Vulture, and Superior Apache tear sources in central Arizona.

Most of the quartz and rhyolite, and much of the other igneous material, was available within the project area, white quartz in particular. Reddish-tan rhyolite also occurs on the surface in several parts of the area. A significant amount of prehistoric procurement and testing took place in the open area between Sites AZ T:3:52(ASM) and AZ T:3:53(ASM) (Figure 1.1).

Table 4.1. Flaked Stone Analysis Summary

Form/Tool Type	Utilization Evidence						Material							
	Scraping	Cutting	Chopping	Pounding	Rubbing	**Total**	Chert	Chal-cedony	Meta-morphic	Quartz	Rhyolite/Igneous	Obsidian	Other	**Total**
Unmodified Piece				8	6	**14**			8	4			4	**16**
Core	2		7	4		**13**	2		2	26	6		2	**38**
Core Fragment	2		9	22	3	**36**	6		8	120	10		13	**157**
Shatter	1			14	1	**16**	29	4	14	269	23	1	43	**383**
Exterior Flake	9	1	2	6	1	**19**	16	2	4	47	39		37	**145**
Interior Flake	27	2		5	1	**35**	76	18	11	78	64	7	58	**312**
Pounding Stone	1		2	20		**23**				12	2		7	**21**
Chopper	1		9			**10**			1	4	4		3	**12**
Scraper Plane	2					**2**					2			**2**
Scraper	5					**5**	1			1	3		4	**9**
Flake Scraper	14					**14**	4	1		1	11		4	**21**
Biface Knife		8				**8**	5	2	1		3			**11**
Thinning Flake						**0**	1	2			1	2	2	**8**
Resharpening Flake		1				**1**	1							**1**
Flake Knife	1	4				**5**					1	1	2	**4**
Thick Biface	2	1				**3**	1	1			5			**7**
Drill					1	**1**	1					1		**2**
Projectile Point		1				**1**	3					1	1	**5**
Pressure Flake						**0**	1	1						**2**
Rubbing Stone					1	**1**							1	**1**
Total	**67**	**18**	**29**	**79**	**14**	**207**	**147**	**31**	**49**	**562**	**174**	**13**	**181**	**1157**

Table 4.2. Flaked Stone Analysis, AZ T:3:41(ASM)

Form/Tool Type	Utilization Evidence						Material							
	Scraping	Cutting	Chopping	Pounding	Rubbing	Total	Chert	Chal-cedony	Meta-morphic	Quartz	Rhyolite/ Igneous	Obsidian	Other	Total
Unmodified Piece				4	1	5			3				2	5
Core			3	1		4				13			1	14
Core Fragment			3	14	3	20	1		6	49	1		3	60
Shatter				1		1	2	1	1	65		1	8	78
Exterior Flake				2	1	3	1	1	2	12	2		6	24
Interior Flake	4				1	5	5	3		22		1	11	42
Pounding Stone				1		1				1				1
Chopper	1		1			2				1	1		1	3
Scraper Plane	1					1					1			1
Scraper	2					2				1			1	2
Flake Scraper	1					1		1						1
Biface Knife						0								0
Thinning Flake						0								0
Resharpening Flake						0								0
Flake Knife						0								0
Thick Biface						0								0
Drill						0								0
Projectile Point						0								0
Pressure Flake						0								0
Rubbing Stone						0								0
Total	9	0	7	23	6	45	9	6	12	164	5	2	33	231

Table 4.3. Flaked Stone Analysis, AZ T:3:42(ASM), Grid and Flat

Form/Tool Type	Utilization Evidence						Material							
	Scraping	Cutting	Chopping	Pounding	Rubbing	**Total**	Chert	Chal-cedony	Meta-morphic	Quartz	Rhyolite/ Igneous	Obsidian	Other	**Total**
Unmodified Piece				3		**3**				2			1	**3**
Core	1		4	2		**7**	1			11	5			**17**
Core Fragment			1			**1**	1			11	1		4	**17**
Shatter				2		**2**	7			39			7	**53**
Exterior Flake	3					**3**	6			9	12		11	**38**
Interior Flake	7	1		2		**10**	22	1	5	15	9		14	**66**
Pounding Stone			1	10		**11**				8			2	**10**
Chopper			4			**4**					3		1	**4**
Scraper Plane						**0**								**0**
Scraper	1					**1**							1	**1**
Flake Scraper	8					**8**	2			1	4		2	**9**
Biface Knife		3				**3**	1		1		2			**4**
Thinning Flake						**0**								**0**
Resharpening Flake						**0**								**0**
Flake Knife	1	1				**2**					1			**1**
Thick Biface	1					**1**					3			**3**
Drill						**0**								**0**
Projectile Point		1				**1**	2							**2**
Pressure Flake						**0**								**0**
Rubbing Stone						**0**								**0**
Total	**22**	**6**	**10**	**19**	**0**	**57**	**42**	**1**	**6**	**96**	**40**	**0**	**43**	**228**

Table 4.4. Flaked Stone Analysis, AZ T:3:42(ASM), Shelter 1

Form/Tool Type	Utilization Evidence						Material							
	Scraping	Cutting	Chopping	Pounding	Rubbing	Total	Chert	Chal-cedony	Meta-morphic	Quartz	Rhyolite/ Igneous	Obsidian	Other	Total
Unmodified Piece				1	1	**2**			2	2				**4**
Core	1					**1**	1		2					**3**
Core Fragment	2		3	6		**11**			2	29			4	**35**
Shatter				8	1	**9**	7		10	77	19		21	**134**
Exterior Flake	2		1	1		**4**	5	1	1	3	9		12	**31**
Interior Flake	6			1		**7**	4	1	5	7	18	1	20	**56**
Pounding Stone				2		**2**				1			2	**3**
Chopper			1			**1**				1				**1**
Scraper Plane						**0**								**0**
Scraper						**0**								**0**
Flake Scraper	2					**2**	1				1		1	**3**
Biface Knife						**0**	1							**1**
Thinning Flake						**0**		1						**1**
Resharpening Flake		1				**1**	1							**1**
Flake Knife		3				**3**						1	2	**3**
Thick Biface						**0**								**0**
Drill					1	**1**	1					1		**2**
Projectile Point						**0**							1	**1**
Pressure Flake						**0**		1						**1**
Rubbing Stone					1	**1**							1	**1**
Total	**13**	**4**	**5**	**19**	**4**	**45**	**21**	**4**	**22**	**120**	**47**	**3**	**64**	**281**

Table 4.5. Flaked Stone Analysis, AZ T:3:42(ASM), Shelter 2

Form/Tool Type	Utilization Evidence						Material							
	Scraping	Cutting	Chopping	Pounding	Rubbing	**Total**	Chert	Chal-cedony	Meta-morphic	Quartz	Rhyolite/ Igneous	Obsidian	Other	**Total**
Unmodified Piece						**0**								**0**
Core						**0**								**0**
Core Fragment			2	1		**3**				7	1			**8**
Shatter				1		**1**	6	1	3	43	2		1	**56**
Exterior Flake			1			**1**	3		1	3			2	**9**
Interior Flake	1	1				**2**	12		1	4	3	5	3	**28**
Pounding Stone				1		**1**				1				**1**
Chopper			1			**1**			1					**1**
Scraper Plane						**0**								**0**
Scraper						**0**								**0**
Flake Scraper						**0**								**0**
Biface Knife		1				**1**		1						**1**
Thinning Flake						**0**						2	2	**4**
Resharpening Flake						**0**								**0**
Flake Knife						**0**								**0**
Thick Biface						**0**								**0**
Drill						**0**								**0**
Projectile Point						**0**						1		**1**
Pressure Flake						**0**	1							**1**
Rubbing Stone						**0**								**0**
Total	**1**	**2**	**4**	**3**	**0**	**10**	**22**	**2**	**6**	**58**	**6**	**8**	**8**	**110**

Table 4.6. Flaked Stone Analysis, AZ T:3:43(ASM)

Form/Tool Type	Utilization Evidence						Material							
	Scraping	Cutting	Chopping	Pounding	Rubbing	Total	Chert	Chal-cedony	Meta-morphic	Quartz	Rhyolite/ Igneous	Obsidian	Other	Total
Unmodified Piece					1	1			1					1
Core						0							1	1
Core Fragment						0	4			8	3		2	17
Shatter	1			1		2	6	1		11	1			19
Exterior Flake	3			1		4	1			9	6		3	19
Interior Flake	7			2		9	29	13		19	18		3	82
Pounding Stone	1			3		4					2		1	3
Chopper			1			1							1	1
Scraper Plane	1					1					1			1
Scraper						0	1							1
Flake Scraper	2					2					4		1	5
Biface Knife		4				4	2	1			1			4
Thinning Flake						0	1	1			1			3
Resharpening Flake						0								0
Flake Knife						0								0
Thick Biface	1	1				2	1	1			2			4
Drill						0								0
Projectile Point						0	1							1
Pressure Flake						0								0
Rubbing Stone						0								0
Total	16	5	1	7	1	30	46	17	1	47	39	0	12	162

Table 4.7. Flaked Stone Analysis, AZ T:3:46(ASM)

Form/Tool Type	Utilization Evidence						Material							
	Scraping	Cutting	Chopping	Pounding	Rubbing	**Total**	Chert	Chal-cedony	Meta-morphic	Quartz	Rhyolite/Igneous	Obsidian	Other	**Total**
Unmodified Piece					1	**1**			1					**1**
Core						**0**				1				**1**
Core Fragment						**0**				11				**11**
Shatter						**0**		1		9			1	**11**
Exterior Flake				2		**2**				7			1	**8**
Interior Flake						**0**				1				**1**
Pounding Stone			1	1		**2**							1	**1**
Chopper						**0**								**0**
Scraper Plane						**0**								**0**
Scraper	1					**1**							1	**1**
Flake Scraper						**0**								**0**
Biface Knife						**0**								**0**
Thinning Flake						**0**								**0**
Resharpening Flake						**0**								**0**
Flake Knife						**0**								**0**
Thick Biface						**0**								**0**
Drill						**0**								**0**
Projectile Point						**0**								**0**
Pressure Flake						**0**								**0**
Rubbing Stone						**0**								**0**
Total	**1**	**0**	**1**	**3**	**1**	**6**	**0**	**1**	**1**	**29**	**0**	**0**	**4**	**35**

Table 4.8. Flaked Stone Analysis, AZ T:3:52(ASM)

Form/Tool Type	Utilization Evidence						Material							
	Scraping	Cutting	Chopping	Pounding	Rubbing	**Total**	Chert	Chal-cedony	Meta-morphic	Quartz	Rhyolite/ Igneous	Obsidian	Other	**Total**
Unmodified Piece					2	**2**			1				1	**2**
Core				1		**1**				1	1			**1**
Core Fragment				1		**1**				5	4			**9**
Shatter				1		**1**	1			25	1		5	**32**
Exterior Flake	1	1				**2**				4	10		2	**16**
Interior Flake	2					**2**	4			10	16		7	**37**
Pounding Stone				2		**2**				1			1	**2**
Chopper			1			**1**				2				**2**
Scraper Plane						**0**								**0**
Scraper	1					**1**					3		1	**4**
Flake Scraper	1					**1**	1				2			**3**
Biface Knife						**0**	1							**1**
Thinning Flake						**0**								**0**
Resharpening Flake						**0**								**0**
Flake Knife						**0**								**0**
Thick Biface						**0**								**0**
Drill						**0**								**0**
Projectile Point						**0**								**0**
Pressure Flake						**0**								**0**
Rubbing Stone						**0**								**0**
Total	**5**	**1**	**1**	**5**	**2**	**14**	**7**	**0**	**1**	**48**	**37**	**0**	**17**	**110**

CHAPTER 5

GROUND STONE ANALYSIS

Arthur W. Vokes

During data recovery four of the prehistoric sites produced ground stone artifacts. Virtually all were metates and manos or milling stones and handstones.

SITE ASSEMBLAGES

AZ T:3:41(ASM)

The excavators recovered a single handstone and several metate fragments from this site (Table 5.1). The handstone was a complete cobble specimen with a somewhat oval shape and only one grinding surface, although other surfaces showed extensive pecking. The ground surface exhibited extensive wear, indicating considerable use. The opposite surface was highly convex and therefore unsuited for grinding use. The cobble did not appear to have required extensive modification prior to use; the pecking may have been done to facilitate handling rather than to change the shape of the artifact.

Three metate fragments found on the surface within and adjacent to Feature 1 were of the same basalt and probably were once parts of a single trough metate; however, the analyst could not refit any of the pieces. Judging from the fragments, the parent metate must have been well shaped and quite large, approximately 11 cm in thickness with a trough at least 5 cm deep.

Nothing indicated an association between the handstone and the metate. The two implements were separated by a distance of 45 m, and the grinding surface of the mano was flat, with none of the polishing along the edges often found on manos extensively used with trough metates.

Table 5.1. Ground Stone Artifacts, AZ T:3:41(ASM)

Artifact	Unit	Material	C/F	Ground Surfaces	Peck	Batter	L	W	T
Mano[1]	N5.6, E62.20	Vesicular basalt	C	1	X	-	10.9	9.5	7.0
Trough metate[2]	Feature 1	Vesicular basalt	F	1	X	-	-	-	-
Trough metate[2]	S10, E20 NE¼	Vesicular basalt	F	1	-	-	-	-	-
Trough metate[2]	S10, E30	Vesicular basalt	F	1	-	-	-	-	-

Note: All artifacts recovered from surface. [1]unground surface pecked [2]probably fragments of a single metate
C=complete; F=fragment; L=length; W=width; T=thickness

AZ T:3:42(ASM)

This site yielded the largest collection of ground stone (n=23), including one stationary boulder. The portable artifact assemblage (Table 5.2) included both complete and fragmentary artifacts. Metates included one complete specimen and five fragments. The complete metate was a slab of fine-grained igneous rock, possibly andesite, ground on both sides. One side was an extensively ground basin metate. A portion of the outer edge was pecked and shaped, and the surface surrounding the basin was extensively pecked and shaped, creating an even, flat surface along one side. The opposite face of the slab was ground as well, less intensively than the basin side but more than necessary for simple shaping, suggesting use as a slab metate.

The five metate fragments represented several different forms. One was part of a well-formed trough metate, while another was probably from a slab metate. The other pieces did not retain sufficient diagnostic attributes to determine form; however, their concave ground surfaces indicated that they were metate fragments, apparently from one artifact, as they were in close proximity to one another when found. The single trough metate fragment indicated that the original implement was extensively shaped, with a deep trough and well-formed walls. All of these specimens were of vesicular basalt. The assemblage also included a large piece of coarse-grained sandstone conglomerate with one relatively fine grained surface used as a grinding slab. This specimen may have been complete, although the margins of the piece were very irregular and not worked in any way. The material was the same as that forming the site shelters, and it is probable that this item was a section of roof fall that the inhabitants of the shelter used briefly and then discarded. This was the only grinding slab or metate section recovered from within a shelter.

Using the criteria developed by Haury (1976) for distinguishing between manos and handstones, the ground stone from Site AZ T:3:42(ASM) included seven manos and three handstones. All the manos were of basalt, some of it vesicular, and had been formally shaped by pecking and grinding. Most exhibited moderate to heavy use. Four showed use wear on two surfaces; in these specimens, one surface generally showed more extensive grinding polish than the other. This group included the smaller specimens, which were ovate in form. The other three manos in the assemblage were more rectangular. One specimen, a reworked section of a trough metate, was unusually broad, with a rectangular block shape, possibly because of its somewhat unusual source. The grinding surface of two of the longer manos wrapped around the ends, indicating use with trough metates. All but one of the manos recovered appeared completely finished. The exception, the specimen made from a metate, showed extensive use on the grinding surface, but the remaining surfaces retained the flake scarring associated with extensive pecking and battering.

Following Haury's (1976) definition, a handstone is a cobble that required little or no modification for grinding use. Two of the three handstones recovered, one of vesicular basalt and the other of an aphanitic igneous rock, were relatively small. The larger third specimen was of gneiss. The two smaller specimens appeared to be stream cobbles and exhibited moderate wear; the larger one was much more irregular and weathered and was ground only on its high points, suggesting minimal use.

This collection included several other artifact classes. A fragment of granite found in the upper levels of Shelter 2 with a small ground area on one flat surface was probably an abrader. An unidentifiable artifact recovered from Shelter 1 was an elongated, worn fragment of fine schist, battered at both ends and with one ground surface. Its trapezoidal cross section was apparently its natural shape. The analysts of similar artifacts recovered from a Sacaton phase pit house at Frogtown, a large hamlet on the

Table 5.2. Ground Stone Artifacts, AZ T:3:42(ASM)

Artifact	Unit	Level[1]	Material	C/F	Ground Surfaces	Peck	Batter	L	W	T
Metate/unknown	S10 E20	0	Vesicular basalt	F	2	-	-	-	-	-
Basin/slab metate	S20 E0	0	Andesite?	C	2	X	-	38.0	26.0	7.0
Metate/unknown	S20 E10	0	Vesicular basalt	F	1	X	-	-	-	-
Unknown form	S20 E10	0	Vesicular basalt (scoria)	F	1	-	-	-	-	-
Metate/unknown	S20 E20	0	Vesicular basalt	F	1	X	-	-	-	-
Rectangular mano (ends ground)	PL 1	0	Basalt	C	1	X	-	16.6	7.9	4.0
Unknown form (heavy use)	PL 7	0	Vesicular basalt	F	1	-	-	-	-	-
Rectangular mano (ends ground)	PL 10	0	Vesicular basalt	C	1	X	-	16.7	10.6	8.1
Oval mano	PL 12	0	Vesicular basalt	F	2	-	-	-	-	-
Rectangular mano	PL 13	0	Basalt	C	2	X	-	11.0	9.0	5.7
Slab (?) metate	PL 15	0	Vesicular basalt	F	1	X	-	-	-	-
Handstone (stream cobble)	PL 16	0	Igneous	C	1	-	-	9.9	7.5	3.7
Trough metate (well shaped)	PL 22	0	Vesicular basalt	F	1	X	-	-	-	-
Oval mano	PL 25	0	Basalt	F	2	X	-	-	-	-
Unknown form (heavy use)	PL 25	0	Basalt	F	1	-	-	-	-	-
Handstone	Shelter 1	0-10	Vesicular basalt	F	1	-	-	-	-	-
Grinding slab	Shelter 1	20-30	Sandstone	F	1	X	X	-	-	-
Rectangular mano	Shelter 1	20-30	Vesicular basalt	C	2	X	-	17.6	13.1	6.6
Rectangular mano (heavy use on trough metate)	Shelter 1	30-40	Basalt	C	1	X	-	18.3	7.2	6.5
Unknown form	Shelter 1	30-40	Schist	C	1	X	X	8.9	1.4	-
Abrader	Shelter 2	0-10	Granite	F	1	-	-	-	-	-
Handstone	Shelter 2	20-30	Gneiss	C	1	-	-	22.5	8.5	7.8

[1]cm below ground surface C=complete; F=fragment; L=length; W=width; T=thickness; PL=point-located artifact

Queen Creek Delta (Bernard-Shaw 1984), suggested that they might have been rasps of some kind. The edges of the Hieroglyphic Mountains specimen, however, did not exhibit the type of wear one might expect from rasping use.

Three ground stone fragments of unidentifiable form came from the surface of the site. All were basalt, with grinding wear on one surface; it is likely that they were fragments of either manos or metates. In addition to the portable artifacts, a large, stationary roof fall boulder found at the front of Shelter 2 exhibited a single grinding area. (This item is not included in Table 5.2.)

In general, the assemblage from Site AZ T:3:42(ASM) was fairly diverse. Many of the specimens showed some degree of shaping, and on several it was quite extensive. Use wear was for the most part moderate to heavy, suggesting extended or repeated periods of use.

AZ T:3:43(ASM)

Excavators recovered only two pieces of ground stone from this site, a complete mano and a fragment of a metate, both of vesicular basalt (Table 5.3). The form of the metate, found in Feature 1 at 10-20 cm below ground level, could not be identified or measured because of its fragmentary state. Its base had been shaped by pecking, and the grinding surface showed extensive use wear. The roughly rectangular mano exhibited some shaping. Both surfaces had been ground, one extensively and the other moderately. This specimen was small compared to manos from other project sites, measuring 13.2 × 8.4 × 4.9 cm. One additional item of ground stone recorded at this site was a large, nonportable basalt boulder with a single oval grinding area.

AZ T:3:52(ASM)

Of the 10 pieces of ground stone recovered during the investigations at this site (Table 5.3), 8 were either complete metates or metate fragments. All complete specimens were on the surface, two of them within the overhang of the shelter. Three of the fragments were from the excavated portion of the shelter. The analyst could not determine the original shape of the fragments. One appeared to be part of a basin or slab metate. All of the complete specimens were blocks of rock with no evidence of shaping. The grinding surfaces did not reflect extensive use. One specimen exhibited only high-point grinding, while the others showed light to moderate use.

The single handstone, recovered from the open surface in front of the shelter, was a natural cobble of vesicular basalt with one grinding surface. The tenth ground stone specimen was a fragmentary piece of vesicular basalt recovered from Level 4, the basal level of the shelter excavation. This piece was too fragmentary to permit identification.

AZ T:3:46(ASM)

The survey team collected one additional ground stone artifact, a bird pendant of ground slate, from this site, a sherd and lithic scatter. The pendant measured approximately 2.3 cm in length by 0.9 cm in

Table 5.3. Ground Stone Artifacts, Site AZ T:3:52(ASM)

Artifact	Unit	Level[1]	Material	C/F	Ground Surfaces	Peck	Batter	L	W	T
Handstone	S20 E40 NE¼	0	Vesicular basalt	C	1	-	-	13.6	10.3	5.8
Slab metate	S30 E40 NE¼	0	Rhyolite	C	1	-	-	40.0	27.0	12.0
Basin metate	S30 E40 NE¼	0	Basalt	C	1	X	-	48.0	32.0	10.0
Slab metate	Shelter	0	Rhyolite	C	1	-	-	36.0	32.0	8.5
Slab metate	Shelter	0	Basalt	C	1	X	-	42.5	31.0	10.5
Metate/unknown	Shelter	0	Igneous	F	1	-	-	-	-	-
Metate/unknown	Shelter	10-20	Igneous	F	1	-	-	-	-	-
Metate/unknown (basin or slab)	Shelter	10-20	Vesicular basalt	F	1	-	-	-	-	-
Metate/unknown	Shelter	20-30	Basalt	F	1	-	-	-	-	-
Unknown form	Shelter	30-40	Vesicular basalt	F	1	-	-	-	-	-

[1]=cm below ground surface   C=complete; F=fragment; L=length; W=width; T=thickness

width and had a drilled hole centered longitudinally about 0.3 cm from the top margin. This artifact was not included in the ground stone analysis, but it is illustrated in Figure 4.11.

SUMMARY

The project sites contained relatively few formal ground stone implements. Efforts to shape the grinding stones were often minimal. Exceptions, in the assemblage at Site AZ T:3:42(ASM), included a number of both manos and metates with extensive pecking and flaking. One specimen appeared to have been in the process of being shaped when it was abandoned, even though it had seen considerable use in this condition. Generally, the materials from this site suggested intensive use histories. The majority of the ground stone artifacts were of igneous material, most frequently vesicular basalt. The source of this material is unknown and may well have been local; none of it appeared to have been from the New River sources (Hoffman and Doyel 1985; Schaller 1985).

It is interesting that all of the complete metates were either basin or slab forms that showed little shaping, while only fragments of a trough metate were present. It is possible that the inhabitants valued the formally shaped trough metates more and did not leave these artifacts behind as they moved about. Other possibilities are that they rarely brought in trough metates from production locations because of their weight or that they did not allocate time to producing these artifacts in the site area.

Since the majority of the ground stone was from the surface of the sites, the analyst was not able to attribute temporal or cultural affiliations to these artifacts beyond what is known for the site as a whole. Unfortunately, the two sites with the largest assemblages, AZ T:3:42(ASM) and AZ T:3:52(ASM), contained evidence of multiple occupations by different cultural groups.

CHAPTER 6

HISTORIC ARTIFACTS

Darbi M. Rea

METHODS

Refuse left behind by miners at Sites AZ T:3:45(ASM) and AZ T:3:48(ASM) provided information concerning the activities conducted at these sites and the periods of occupation or use. Sources from which chronological and functional information was obtained include studies by Busch (1981), Gillio, Levine, and Scott (1980), Kendrick (1963), Rock (1984), Simonis (1988), and Toulouse (1969, 1971).

Attributes such as color, form, label style, and manufacturer's marks allowed the analyst to make temporal and functional inferences about many of the glass artifacts. Attributes of tin cans such as size and manufacturing technology aided in temporal placement, and can form and any modifications contributed to functional determinations (for instance, cans opened by thin opposing slits were assumed to have contained a beverage rather than solid food).

Chronologically sensitive changes in evaporated milk cans from 1875 until the present are well documented (Simonis 1988) and formed an important basis for dating the sites. Evaporated milk is considered to have been a dietary staple of early miners because of its long shelf life and variety of uses. Milk cans constituted the majority (60%) of all containers from AZ T:3:48(ASM) and a large portion (19%) of containers from AZ T:3:45(ASM).

SITE ASSEMBLAGES

AZ T:3:45(ASM)

Artifacts recovered from Loci B and C at Site AZ T:3:45(ASM) indicated that the initial occupation of Locus B may have begun prior to World War I, possibly as early as 1885, and probably was of limited duration (Figure 6.1; Tables 6.1 and 6.2). Locus B was occupied again in the 1920s before the Depression era. Locus C had a brief occupation circa 1915. The limited amount of material deposited at the site suggested that all three occupational episodes were of limited duration and intensity.

The diet of site inhabitants included canned food and milk. Sardines seem to have been a particularly important dietary element. The earlier component of Locus B was notably lacking in remains associated with such indulgences as tobacco, alcoholic beverages, and soda waters. It is not known whether the possible tent base at Locus B was associated with the earlier or the later occupation. The single personal item was a rusted Levi's button found within the structure outline.

The remains from Locus A, Locus C, and the later period at Locus B appeared to be contemporaneous with the increase in metals production between World War I and the Depression. Locus C, dating to circa 1915, could conceivably have been contemporaneous with the later component of Locus B. However, the

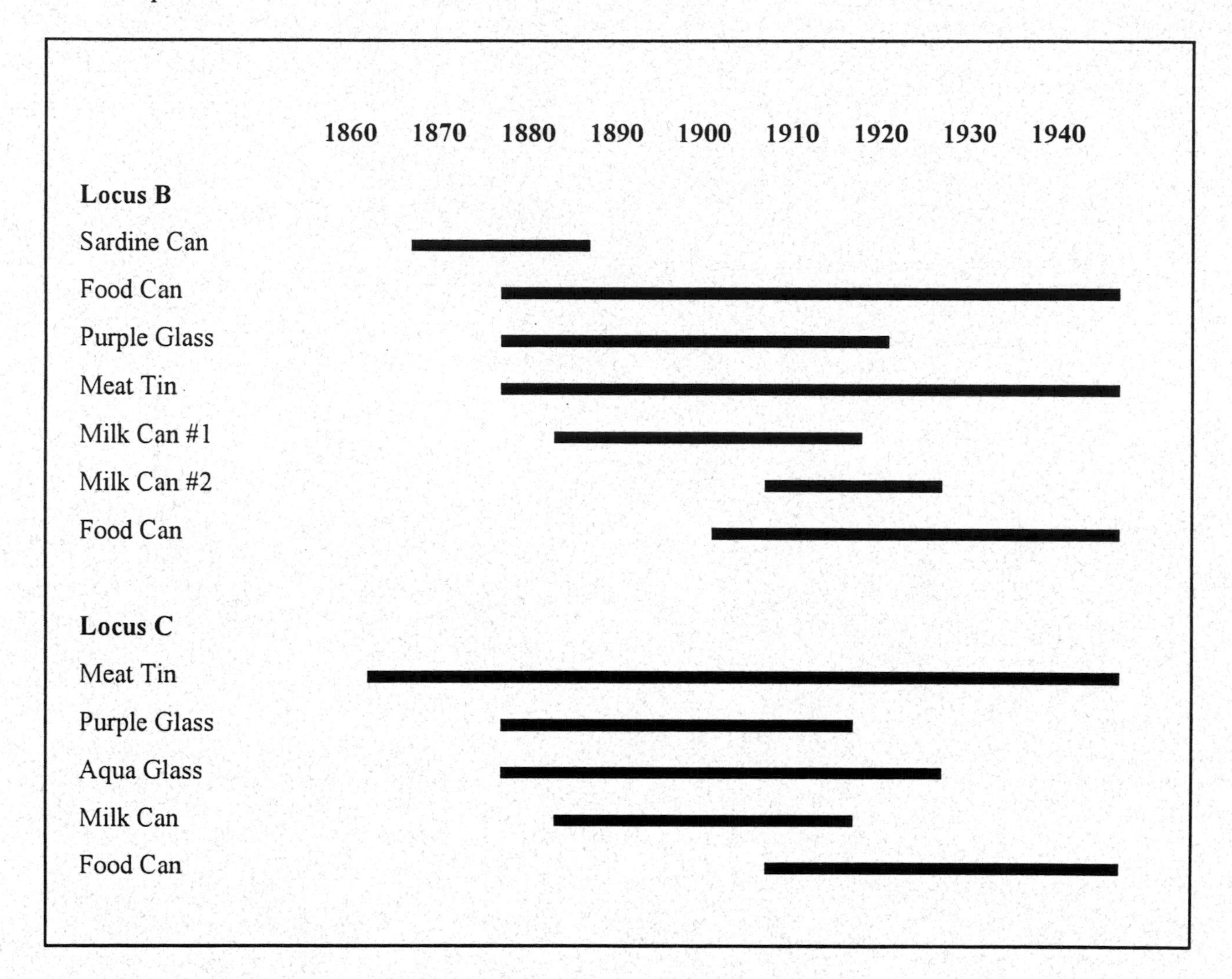

Figure 6.1. AZ T:3:45(ASM), dates of manufacture of historic artifacts.

meat tins and other associated artifacts from Locus C appeared to be earlier, and it seems doubtful that two separate camp areas would have been simultaneously maintained for such a small operation. The 1920s component at Locus B produced the greatest number of artifacts of the site components and presumably represented the longest or most intensive occupation. The mine shaft at Locus A appeared on the 1922 General Land Office map.

AZ T:3:48(ASM)

Artifacts from Site AZ T:3:48(ASM) suggested two periods of occupation or use, one between 1915 and 1935 and the second between 1950 and 1960 (Figure 6.2; Tables 6.3A–D and 6.4). Government controls and assistance legislation just prior to the Depression, as well as advances in mining technology, made processing of low-grade ores profitable, and the earlier occupation may have been related to the increase in mining activity that resulted. The later and relatively smaller occupation may have been

Table 6.1. AZ T:3:45(ASM), Locus B, Historic Artifacts

Type	Description*	End Seam	Side Seam	TN	MNA	Date
Tin Can						
Evaporated milk 1[a]	2-15/16 × 4-6/16 × 1-9/16[b]	S	S	12	12	1885–1908
Evaporated milk 2	2-15/16 × 3-5/16, none	C	C	4	4	1914–1930
Food	4-8/16 × 3-6/16 × 1-7/16	C	C	13	13	1880–1930
Food	3 × 4-9/16, matchstick	C	S	4	4	
Food	2-9/16 × 4 × 1-1/2	C	C	4	4	1880–1930
Food	3-6/16 × 9/16, none	C	C	1	1	
Food	4 × 4-11/16 × 2-9/16	C	C	7	7	1880–1930
Food	3-9/16 × 1-12/16, matchstick	C	C	1	1	
Food	5-14/16 × 2-12/16 ?	C	C	1	1	
Food	3-14/16 × 3-4/16 ?	C	C	2	2	
Food	4 × 3-3/16 × 2	C	C	3	3	1880–1930
Food	? × 6-2/16 ?	C	C	1	1	
Food	3 × 4-7/16, matchstick	C	C	1	1	
Food	4 × 2-10/16 × 1-10/16	C	C	1	1	1880–1930
Baking powder ?		C	C	1	1	
Coffee		C	C	1	1	
Lard bucket ?		C	C	1	1	
Sardine	3 piece	S	S	21	21	1830–1880
Meat	tapered shape, 1-10/16 cap	C	S	13	13	
Spice	Schilling's Best, 16-oz lid	?	?	1	1	
Tin can lid	5 sizes			14		
Glass						
Clear	pane, thin			2	1	
Light green				48	1	
Purple				2	1	1880–1915
Brown				6	1	
Miscellaneous						
Shotgun shell	Winchester No. 10, New Rival			1	1	
Machinery metal	3/16 × 4-1/4 × 1-12/16			1	1	
Metal scrap				101		
Wood scrap				4		
Button	Levi's			1	1	

*All measurements in inches.
TN=total number of pieces; MNA=minimum number of artifacts; S=soldered; C=crimped
[a]Milk cans numbered chronologically [b]diameter × height × cap size

Table 6.2. AZ T:3:45(ASM), Locus C, Historic Artifacts

Type	Description*			TN	MNA	Date
Tin Can		**End Seam**	**Side Seam**			
Evaporated milk	2-15/16 × 4-7/16 × 1-9/16[a]	C	S	3	3	1885–1908
Food	2-15/16 × 4-11/16, matchstick	C	S	1	1	
Food	4 × 3-3/16 × 2-4/16	C	C	1	1	
Meat	tapered shape	C	S	5	5	1820–1930
Sardine	3-1/16 × 4-4/16 × 1	C	S	2	2	
Tobacco	hinged top	C	C	1	1	
Glass and Ceramics						
Glass	clear, patinated			30	1	
Bottle	purple, small			1	1	1880–1915
Bottle	aqua, panel			4	1	1880–1920
Porcelain	yellow on white			29	1	
Miscellaneous						
Machinery metal				8	1	
Metal scrap				34	1	

*All measurements in inches
TN=total number of pieces; MNA=minimum number of artifacts; S=soldered; C=crimped
[a]diameter × height × cap size

associated with efforts to "clean up" the mine. AZ T:3:48(ASM) was probably a small operation of one to three individuals during each of the occupations represented. Artifacts relating to both temporal components were present in Trash Cluster A, while Trash Cluster B contained only 1920s materials. Milk cans of pre-Depression styles constituted 58% of all metal containers at AZ T:3:48(ASM).

Provisions

The miners at Site AZ T:3:48(ASM) subsisted on a diet that included milk, meat, fish, fruits, and vegetables. Not unexpectedly, they appeared to have been largely dependent on canned and preserved foods. The presence of a number of baking powder cans indicated that they prepared baked goods as well. Among the milk containers identified, only two were bottles. Tinned meats included products from both Uruguay and Argentina, and seafood products were both American and Norwegian. Numerous spice and condiment containers were also recovered.

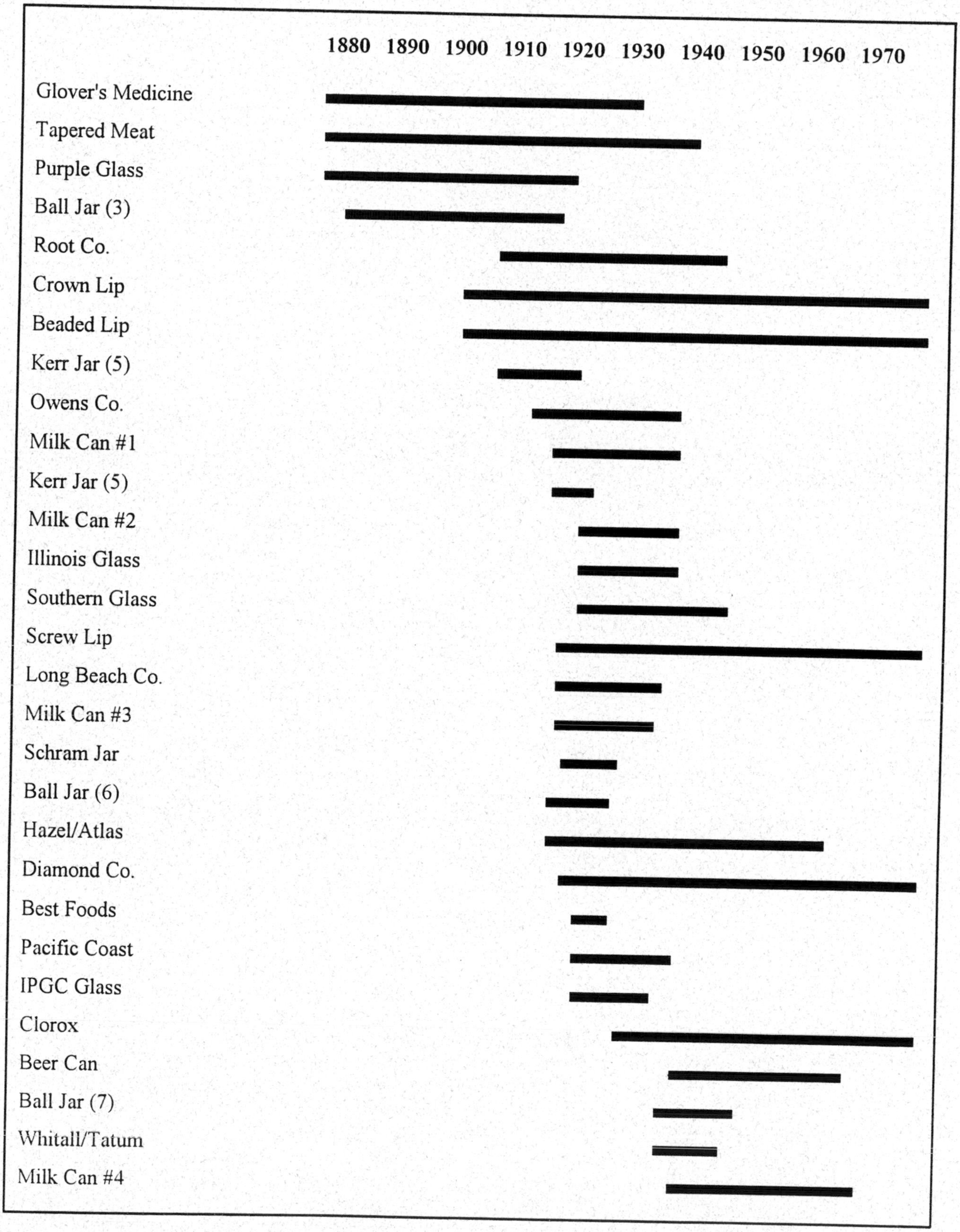

1880 1890 1900 1910 1920 1930 1940 1950 1960 1970

Glover's Medicine
Tapered Meat
Purple Glass
Ball Jar (3)
Root Co.
Crown Lip
Beaded Lip
Kerr Jar (5)
Owens Co.
Milk Can #1
Kerr Jar (5)
Milk Can #2
Illinois Glass
Southern Glass
Screw Lip
Long Beach Co.
Milk Can #3
Schram Jar
Ball Jar (6)
Hazel/Atlas
Diamond Co.
Best Foods
Pacific Coast
IPGC Glass
Clorox
Beer Can
Ball Jar (7)
Whitall/Tatum
Milk Can #4

Figure 6.2. AZ T:3:48(ASM), dates of manufacture of historic artifacts. (Numbers in parentheses refer to type numbers from Toulouse 1969.)

Table 6.3A. AZ T:3:48(ASM), Trash Cluster A, Historic Artifacts: Tin Cans

Type	Description	End Seam	Side Seam	TN	MNA	Date
Evaporated milk 1[a]	4-6/16 × 2-15/16[b], matchstick	C	C	557	557	1915–1930
Evaporated milk 2	4-4/16 × 2-15/16, matchstick	C	C	62	62	1917–1929
Evaporated milk 3	2-7/16 × 2-8/16, matchstick	C	C	164	164	1920–1930
Food	small, 3–4 × 2–3, none	C	S	34	34	1902–1920
Food	small, 3–4 × 2–3, none	C	C	17	17	
Food	medium, 4–4-1/2 × 3–3-6/16	C	S	4	4	
Food	medium, 4–4-1/2 × 3–3-6/16	C	C	32	32	
Food	large, 4-1/2–5 × 3-6/16–4	C	S	38	38	
Food	large, 4-1/2–5 × 3-6/16–4, beverage slits	C	C	175	175	
Food	2–3 × 2–3, with key strips	C	C	11	11	
Food	6-15/16 × 6-3/16	C	C	1	1	
Meat	Uruguay	C	C	1	1	
Meat	Argentina	C	C	1	1	
Meat	Spam type, tapered hole in cap	C	C	13	13	pre-1930
Meat ?	squat, 2-11/16 × 4	C	C	2	2	
Sardines	Norway and U.S.	C	C	5	5	post-1860
Seafood	large, oval	C	C	5	5	
Seafood ?	one with key strip	C	C	12	12	
Lard ?	large, ridged	C	C	6	6	
Coffee	Hills Bros., 1 lb and 1/2 lb	C	C	12	12	
Tea	Lipton, Planter Ceylon	C	C	2	2	
Tea	"Try Tree Tea" lid	C	C	1	1	
Tea	Maxwell House	C	C	1	1	
Spice	oval lid	C	C	12	12	
Spice	large, with sprinkle lid	C	C	12	12	
Baking powder	Calumet, 4 oz, 1 lb, 2-1/2 lb	C	C	5	5	
Pharmaceutical	aspirin-type	C	C	16	16	
Tobacco	Prince Albert	C	C	27	27	
Beer	flat top			5	5	post-1935
Mason jar lid	Kerr wide-mouth and standard			13	13	
Food lid	"Seconds"			1	1	
Food lid	"Sugar Added"			1	1	
Lid	grater or sifter slip on lid			1	1	
Unknown contents	square, 7"			2	2	
Unknown contents	small lid			2	2	
Unknown contents	lid, entire diameter			1	1	
Nonfood	square, 7", circle-in-diamond			2	2	
Nonfood	ridged, writing, machine hole			1	1	
Nonfood	long cans			2	2	
Nonfood	paint type, "Stir Thoroughly"			2	2	
Nonfood	auto fluids			2	2	
Nonfood	square, 9-10/16 × 5-4/16 × 5-4/16			1	1	
Nonfood	Union Carbide markings			4	4	

*All measurements in inches

TN=total number of pieces; MNA=minimum number of artifacts; S=soldered; C = crimped

[a]Milk cans numbered chronologically [B]diameter × height × cap size

Table 6.3B. AZ T:3:48(ASM), Trash Cluster A, Historic Artifacts: Glass

Type	Description	TN	MNA	Dates
Jar	clear, necked rim	2	1	
Jar	clear, large, Best Foods, condiments	1	1	1925–1930
Jar	clear, medium, double ring rim	3	3	
Jar	clear, honeycomb design; honey?	1	1	
Jar	clear, large, screw top rim	1	1	
Jar	clear, small, Best Foods, condiments	1	1	
Jar	dark blue, Vicks	6	1	
Jar	hexagonal rim design	3	1	
Jar	light purple, ?	1	1	1880–1915
Jar, angular strips	0.8-cm fluting	3	1	
Jar, angular strips	2.0-cm fluting	7	1	
Jar, angular strips	1.4-cm fluting, Hazel/Atlas Glass	6	1	1920–1964
Jar, angular strips	1.7-cm fluting	3	1	
Jar, angular strips	pink, 2.6-cm fluting	10	1	
Jar, angular strips	2.2-cm fluting	1	1	
Mason jar	blue, Ball Perfect (6)[a], fruit/vegetable	47	22	1920s
Mason jar	light purple, Glenross ?	4	2	1880–1915
Mason jar	light green, Ball Mason (3), fruit/vegetable	98	2	1895–1910
Mason jar	light blue-green, Ball Perfect (7), fruit/vegetable	2	1	1935
Mason jar	purple, Schram Automatic, fruit/vegetable	7	2	1920–1925
Mason jar	flint, Kerr Self Sealing, fruit/vegetable	13	2	1915
Mason jar	clear, Kerr (5)	1	1	1915–1919
Mason jar	fragments, unknown types	35	3	
Jar (?)	clear, 1.1-cm fluted design	1	1	
Jar lid	clear, small	1	1	
Bottle or Jar	clear, patinated, large	1	1	
Bottle	clear, rectangular	4	1	
Bottle	clear, Owens Co.	1	1	1911–1929
Bottle	clear, Illinois Pacific Glass Co.	2	2	1925–1930
Bottle	clear, Pacific Coast	2	2	1925–1930
Bottle	clear, angular edges	1	1	
Bottle	clear, Diamond Co.	1	1	1924-present
Bottle	clear, crown lip, beverage	1	1	1903-present
Bottle	clear, Long Beach	1	1	1920–1933
Bottle	clear, Hazel/Atlas, beverage	2	2	1920–1964
Bottle, panel	clear, frosted, rectangular	1	1	
Beverage	brown, Beaded Lip	1	1	1903-present
Beverage	brown, Crown Lip (2 types)	2	2	1903-present
Bleach	brown, Clorox	1	1	1929–1962
Milk bottle	clear	1	1	
Nonalcoholic	brown, Southern Glass Co., beverage	4	3	1917–1931
Pharmaceutical	brown, Illinois Glass Co.	1	1	1916–1929
Pharmaceutical	brown, Glovers Imperial Mange Medicine	7	1	1867–1915
Pharmaceutical	brown, Whitall-Tatum	1	1	1935–1938

Table 6.3B. AZ T:3:48(ASM), Trash Cluster A, Historic Artifacts: Glass, continued

Type	Description	TN	MNA	Dates
Soda pop	clear, with designs	4	1	
Soda pop ?	light green, PLUTO, Root Glass Co.	1	1	1903–1932
Soda pop ?	light green, PLUTO top? crown lip	1	1	1903-present
Spice	clear, Ben Hur	1	1	
Unknown	brown fragments	53	1	
Unknown	clear, round bottle bottoms	11	11	
Unknown	clear	3	2	
Unknown	clear fragments	446	6	
Unknown	light purple, with label ...LOTI...	1	1	1880–1915
Unknown	pink tint, line design	26	1	
Unknown	screw-cap lip	1	1	
Bottle top	clear, beaded lip	3	3	
Bottle top	clear, double ring	1	1	
Bottle top	clear, small, beverage, screw cap	3	3	
Bottle top	clear, large, beverage, screw cap	1	1	
Bottle top	clear, triple ring	1	1	
Dessert dish	clear, fluted design	4	1	
Drinking glass	clear, line design rim	2	2	
Drinking glass	purple tint, fluted design	1	1	1880–1915
Drinking glass	flint, plain	1	1	
Measuring cup	clear, 16 oz	8	1	
Car window	green, thick pane, rounded edge	2	1	pre-1928
Car window	blue, thick pane (0.6 cm)	41	1	pre-1928
Car window	blue, thin pane (0.2 cm)	64	1	
Car window	light green, thick pane, flat edge	9	1	pre-1928
Car window	green, thick pane, beveled edge	1	1	pre-1928
Car window	light blue, thick pane (0.5 cm)	7	1	pre-1928
Nondiagnostic	light green, plain	32	1	
Nondiagnostic	pink	23	1	
Nondiagnostic	purple, patinated	3	1	1880–1915

TN = total number of pieces; MNA = minimum number of artifacts
[a]Numbers in parentheses refer to type numbers from Toulouse 1969.

Indulgences

Coffee and tea were the most common non-nutritive consumables represented in the assemblage, and the miners probably considered them an essential part of the daily diet. Remains indicating use of tobacco were also very common. The assemblage contained fewer than 10 soda pop or alcoholic beverage bottles dating before the Depression, although the indistinguishable glass fragments found in the trash heap may have represented additional consumable items. Five beer cans dating to the post-Depression era were near the mine, at some distance from the main dumping area.

Table 6.3C. AZ T:3:48(ASM), Trash Cluster A, Historic Artifacts: Ceramics

Type	Description	TN	MNA
Bowl	porcelain, green with purple flowers	3	1
Bowl, steep	porcelain, green leaf rim design	1	1
Bowl, steep	porcelain, bold striped rim	2	1
Bowl, steep	porcelain, blue baskets and bows	9	1
Bowl, steep	porcelain, blue double-line design	7	1
Bowl, shallow	porcelain, white, elaborate rim design	3	1
Bowl, shallow	porcelain, angular edges, green and purple	6	1
Bowl, shallow	porcelain, blue rim with purple flowers	7	1
Bowl, shallow	porcelain, scalloped blue floral	1	1
Plate	porcelain, white, simple line rim	11	1
Plate	porcelain, gold raised design with pink flowers	11	1
Plate	porcelain, brown floral	4	1
Teacup	porcelain, green fluted	1	1
Teacup	porcelain, Chinese-style scenery	9	1
Teacup	porcelain, gold and pink stripes	5	2
Teacup	porcelain, gold rim	1	1
Teacup	porcelain, blue rim with purple flowers	2	1
Teacup	porcelain, plain white	20	1
Bowl base rim, large	porcelain, chamber pot	20	1
Bowl base, medium	porcelain, 0.55 cm	3	1
Bowl base, small	porcelain, 0.15 cm	3	1
Plain fragment	porcelain, white	179	3
Crockery	stoneware	3	2
Unknown	blue-lined rim	1	1
Nondiagnostic	fragments with design	10	7

TN=total number of pieces; MNA=minimum number of artifacts

Medicines

The most notable medicinal artifact, associated with the earliest occupation, was a panel bottle for "Grover's Imperial Mange Medicine." Mange is a contagious skin disease that affects both humans and domesticated animals. The assemblage included 3 other pharmaceutical bottles and 18 aspirin-type tins.

Domestic Routine

Artifacts associated with food preparation included the body of a small wood stove and three stovepipe fragments, a 16-ounce glass measuring cup, and as many as three large bowls, which could have been used for mixing or serving. Fragments of 8 teacups, 12 bowls, 4 plates, 4 drinking glasses, and 1 dessert dish represented individual dishes. Among the wide assortment of designs observed, only two teacup fragments and two drinking glass fragments showed matching designs. The miners may have used bleach from a

Table 6.3D. AZ T:3:48(ASM), Trash Cluster A, Historic Artifacts: Miscellaneous

Type	Description*	TN	MNA
Nail	2 cut, 28 wire	30	30
Bucket	small, 5-12/16 × 5[a] (not collected)	2	2
Bucket	medium, 6-4/16 × 5-10/16 (not collected)	10	10
Bucket	large, 10-3/16 × 10-7/16 (not collected)	1	1
Bucket	X-large, 13 × 14-1/2 (not collected)	2	2
Galvanized tub	9-15/16 × 22-12/16 (not collected)	1	1
Gas tank	37 × 9 × 16 (not collected)	1	1
Tank (gas?)	29-2/16 × 10 × 12-14/16 (not collected)	1	1
Scrap metal		504	-
Light bulb	standard	2	2
Plastic	white, thin	7	1
Spring	large	1	1
Latch	trunk-style	1	1
Hook	metal, snap strap	1	1
Battery core		3	3
Button	metal, CTA sewn	2	2
Lid	twist-off	1	1
Button	metal, two-hole	1	1
Button	mother-of-pearl	1	1
Boot heel	rubber (made from tire tread), with tacks	1	1
Cap, small	metal, labeled "...Times Daily...drug..."	1	1
Cartridge	30-30	1	1
Shell	Winchester	1	1
Grommet		3	3
Cylindrical object	metal	2	1
Stove parts	metal: body, 3 pieces of stovepipe, wall attachments	6	1
Iron-sharpening scrap		5	1
Pull cork		1	1
Small wheel	door or drawer part?	1	1
Trunk part	with shining star	1	1
Snap-It object	hand-held electrical appliance	6	1
Auto part	solenoid	1	1
Auto window part	rubber, piece of gasket	1	1
Carriage bolt	large	1	1
Ceramic fragment	insulator?	1	1
Machinery strap	metal	2	1
Tool-handle part	metal	2	2
Screen-frame fragment		1	1
Battery	C	3	1
Metal nozzle		1	1
Scrap wire		1	1
Unidentified		2	-

*All measurements in inches [a]diameter × height × cap size
TN=total number of pieces; MNA=minimum number of artifacts

Table 6.4. AZ T:3:48(ASM), Trash Cluster B, Historic Artifacts

Type	Description	End Seam	Side Seam	TN	MNA	Date
Tin Can[a]		**End Seam**	**Side Seam**			
Food	4-1/2 × 3-3/8[b]	C	C	2	2	
Food	4-5/8 × 3	C	C	1	1	
Food	4 × ?	C	C	1	1	
Food	3-1/4 × 2-11/16	C	C	1	1	
Baking powder	Calumet, 1 lb	C	C	1	1	
Coffee	key on bottom	C	C	2	2	
Can base		C	C	1	1	
Aspirin-type	rectangular	-	-	2	2	
Jar lid	Mason	-	-	10	10	
Jar lid	screw-on	-	-	2	2	
Jar lid	press-on	-	-	1	1	
Jar lid	labeled "Poison"	-	-	1	1	
Glass						
Glass fragment	purple	-	-	1	1	1880–1915
Bottle fragment	milk, one labeled	-	-	2	1	
Bottle neck	medicine	-	-	1	1	
Bottle	clear, long neck, screw-on cap	-	-	1	1	
Bottle fragment	clear	-	-	6	1	
Bottle base	Hazel/Atlas	-	-	1	1	1920–1964
Bottle base	"I"	-	-	1	1	
Ceramics						
Teacup	porcelain	-	-	1	1	
Bowl	porcelain	-	-	1	1	
Saucer	porcelain, Gold Medal	-	-	1	1	
Plate	porcelain, Laughlin	-	-	1	1	
Support yoke		-	-	1	1	
Miscellaneous						
Claw-hammer head		-	-	1	1	
Strap piece	1/2, 1-1/2, 2-1/2	-	-	4	1	
Scrap wire piece		-	-	5	1	
Pipe fragment	threaded	-	-	4	1	
Pump hose	brass	-	-	1	1	
Grommet	for canvas	-	-	1	1	
Radio tube	large	-	-	1	1	

*All measurements in inches   [a]includes metal jar lids   [b]diameter × height
TN=total number of pieces; MNA=minimum number of artifacts; C=crimped

recovered Clorox bottle for washing clothes or for sanitizing dishes. Miscellaneous housewares included "C" batteries, standard light bulbs, cores from a large battery, and fragments of window or door screen frames. A large radio tube was found at Trash Cluster B.

Personal Effects

One of the four buttons recovered from AZ T:3:48(ASM) was mother-of-pearl; the other three were metal. Three of four small metal grommets appeared to have been from clothing or shoes. Two recovered trunk pieces were decorated, one with a shining-star emblem. A single boot heel had been fashioned from rubber tire tread and attached with small, square tacks of different sizes.

Transportation

The thick (0.5–0.6 cm) car-window-type glass found at AZ T:3:48(ASM) may have been from the 1920s occupation. This type predates safety glass, which car makers first used in 1928. Associated with the trash dump were one auto gas tank and another tank that may also have been for gas. Also included in the assemblage were one cylindrical solenoid part; a single piece of rubber car-window stripping; and two cone-top tin containers that resembled auto-fluid cans. Some of the unidentifiable nonfood cans may also have held auto fluids. These artifacts could be related to either of the post-1920s occupations.

Construction and Industry

The nonfood cans recovered included four bearing "Union Carbide" markings. One jar lid was labeled "Poison." Of the 30 nails found, two were cut nails, probably dating before 1900, although such nails are still in use for specific tasks. All other specimens were wire nails. Trash Cluster B contained one broken claw-hammer head. The miners could have used the 15 buckets that were present to haul water or transport mineral samples from the shaft. Other industrial items included two metal tool-handle parts used in hafting the end of a shovel or hoe to a cylindrical handle; five small iron chips that appeared to have been produced as a result of sharpening mining picks; metal strap fragments; nuts and bolts; a support yoke; bucket handles; scrap wire; threaded pipe-nozzle fragments; and a brass pump hose and parts.

Miscellaneous and Unidentified Fragments

One artifact labeled "Snap-It" appeared to have been part of a hand-held electrical appliance. Whether it was for industrial or household use is unknown, but it was designed to operate on 125–230 volts. Other miscellaneous objects included a tarp grommet, a burned ceramic electrical insulator fragment, and numerous unidentified metal and plastic fragments.

Summary

Some artifacts recovered from Site AZ T:3:48(ASM) suggested the presence of a habitation structure. These items included two circular, flat pieces of metal that functioned to attach a stovepipe to a wall, standard size light bulbs, window glass, and fragments of window or door screen frames. No other evidence for this structure was present at the site, and the investigators could not determine the kind of structure or its date.

DISCUSSION

The development of mining activities during the late nineteenth and early twentieth centuries provides the best context for understanding historic use of the project area as revealed in the materials discussed above. Table 6.5 summarizes the inferred chronology of the project sites in terms of these developments.

Table 6.5. Inferred Chronology of Historic Sites

Site	Date	National Era	National Resource Priority
AZ T:3:45(ASM)			
Locus A	1920s	post-WWI production	copper or gold
Locus B	circa 1885	railroads, treaties, gold standard	gold, copper, silver
	1920s	post-WWI production	copper or gold
Locus C	circa 1915	WWI buildup	copper
AZ T:3:48(ASM)			
Trash Cluster A	circa 1915	WWI buildup	copper
	1920s	post-WWI production	copper or gold
	1950s	post-WWII production	copper
Trash Cluster B	1920s	post-WWI production	copper or gold

In his history of mining in Arizona, summarized here, Dunning (1966) described the period between 1880 and 1893 as the most significant. Several factors contributed to this mining boom. In 1883 the railroad finally spanned North America, providing easier access and transportation to and from mining areas. In 1886 General Nelson A. Miles secured the surrender of the Apaches, creating a popular perception that Arizona was now a safer place for miners. The Yavapais had been subdued as early as 1873 (Corbusier 1886).

From 1884 to 1893, a battle raged between advocates of a silver standard and the champions of a gold standard. Although silver was important until it was demonetized in 1893, the widespread fear of the unlimited coinage of silver encouraged gold mining. Meanwhile, copper was coming into its own; its price quadrupled between 1880 and 1886 and then doubled again by 1888.

World War I created massive demands for industrial metals such as copper during the period between 1915 and 1918. This mining bonanza crashed abruptly with the end of the war. By 1921 virtually all Arizona mines had closed. Two years later the mines reopened, and production steadily increased until 1929. During the 1930s, the Great Depression drastically affected the mining industry. Large copper mines maintained only skeleton crews, and marginal operations were forced to shut down altogether. Some small gold mines continued operating, however, due to the high price of gold.

During World War II, the U.S. Government shut down all mining that did not pertain to wartime manufacturing. The government also maintained stringent controls on production and pricing prior to and during the war, a policy intended to avert an anticipated postwar crash in the mining industry. Contrary to predictions, however, the United States continued to produce and stockpile armaments in a massive arms race following the war. In addition, the public, following the prolonged period of wartime rationing, began demanding a wide range of consumer items. As a result, copper experienced a controlled but steady growth in production. This trend continued into the next decades, with additional government assistance programs to encourage and sustain the industry.

CHAPTER 7

SUMMARY AND CONCLUSIONS

Donald R. Keller

CHRONOLOGY AND CULTURAL AFFILIATION

Prehistoric and Protohistoric Components

The researchers derived evidence pertaining to the age and culture of the prehistoric sites investigated during this project from three sources: radiocarbon dating, ceramics, and diagnostic projectile points. Considerable mixing of material within and between cultural deposits limited the usefulness of relative dating methods.

Several lines of evidence indicated contextual disturbances. First, rodent burrows occurred throughout the fill. Bits of plastic wrapper were ubiquitous, and a number of uncharred plant seeds from flotation samples bore rodent tooth marks (Appendix C). Field crews observed evidence that larger animals had been digging in the upper fill as well. The second indicator of disturbance was the distribution of ceramics. Sherds from late and early ceramic types occurred together, especially in the lower portions of the deposits, and all levels of the fill from Shelter 1 at Site AZ T:3:42(ASM) contained sherds from a single vessel. Third, the largely undifferentiated ashy nature of the deposits suggested that a certain amount of mixing had taken place during site occupation as a result of foot traffic and fill modification. A rockshelter site (AZ T:3:16[ASM]) just east of the present project area also contained deposits of this type (Gumerman, Weed, and Hanson 1976), which may be typical of shelter deposits in this region.

Because of these problems, analysts could draw only general conclusions regarding the chronological affiliation of the shelters. For example, general periods of occupation might be defined, but associating particular items such as nondiagnostic artifacts or ethnobotanical remains with these periods would be unwarranted. Table 7.1 summarizes the inferred periods of occupation or use of project sites.

Radiocarbon Analysis

Charcoal in the site deposits was common but was small grained and generally very dispersed. Field crews collected three samples from small clusters of charcoal that appeared to be associated. Tables from Klein et al. (1982) (see also Appendix A) were the basis for calibrating the uncorrected dates received from Beta Analytic, Inc. The corrected dates form the basis for the interpretations offered.

The two samples from Site AZ T:3:42(ASM) were from the upper cultural layers of Shelter 1. One sample (Beta 27148) was from the top of the main ashy-gray artifact-rich stratum (10 cm below surface), which underlay the largely sterile surface layer. This sample yielded an uncorrected date of 320 years ± 60 B.P., or A.D. 1570–1690; the two calibrated ranges for this date were A.D. 1422–1658 and A.D. 1484–1678. A second sample (Beta 27149) was from a lower stratigraphic position (25 cm below ground surface), where sterile colluvium from the east end of the shelter intertongued with the upper half of the ashy-gray cultural stratum. This sample yielded a date of 300 years B.P. ± 50, or A.D. 1600–1700; the

Table 7.1. Inferred Periods of Occupation of Project Sites

Site (ASM)	Culture		
	Prehistoric (Hohokam)	Protohistoric (Yavapai)	Historic (Euroamerican)
AZ T:3:41	Sacaton (?) (A.D. 900–1150)		
AZ T:3:42			
Flat	pre-Classic(?) (before A.D. 1150)	1400s–1600s (?)	
Shelter 1	Sacaton, late Classic (A.D. 900–1150; A.D. 1300–1450+)	1400s–1600s (?)	
Shelter 2	Santa Cruz, Sacaton-Soho transition (A.D. 700–900; ± A.D. 1100–1200)		
AZ T:3:43	Sacaton-Soho transition (± A.D. 1100–1200)		
AZ T:3:45			ca. 1885 ca. 1915 1920s
AZ T:3:46	pre-Classic (before A.D. 1150)		
AZ T:3:48			ca. 1915 1920s 1950s
AZ T:3:52	Sacaton, Soho (A.D. 900–1200)	1400s–1700s (?)	

calibrated range for this date was A.D. 1430–1660 (Klein et al. 1982). The sample from Site AZ T:3:52 (ASM) (Beta 27150) was from a small ash and charcoal lens in the uppermost part of the cultural stratum (5 cm below in the uppermost part of the cultural stratum (5 cm below ground surface). This sample provided a date of 270 years B.P. ± 50 years, or a range of A.D. 1630–1730; the two calibrated ranges for this sample were A.D. 1485–1665 and A.D. 1760–1795.

Given the disturbed nature of the deposits, a cautious and general interpretation of these dates suggests that human use of the shelters occurred sometime between the fifteenth and eighteenth centuries. Analysts were not able to correlate these dates with particular deposits or materials contained within them.

Ceramic Dating

Vokes (Chapter 3) has discussed in detail the chronological information provided by the project ceramics. In summary, his analysis indicated that the Hohokam occupied or used Site AZ T:3:41(ASM) during the Sedentary period. Site AZ T:3:42(ASM) produced the most varied ceramic assemblage, representing a time span from the Hohokam Colonial period through the remainder of the prehistoric era and possibly persisting into the Historic period.

The material from Shelter 1 at Site AZ T:3:42(ASM) included sherds dated to the Hohokam Sedentary period and types diagnostic of late Classic period Hohokam ceramic assemblages (Tonto Polychrome, Jeddito Black-on-yellow). Other sherds recovered were a pot break representing a Tizon Wiped vessel, found approximately 50 m north of Shelter 1, and four sherds of what may have been Apache-affiliated plainware, found within the shelter.

Shelter 2 contained Santa Cruz Red-on-buff sherds, indicating use of the shelter as early as the Colonial period. Ceramic evidence also suggested that Hohokam groups used the shelter during the Sedentary-to-Classic transition and perhaps again during the Classic period.

Site AZ T:3:43(ASM) also appeared to have been occupied during the Sedentary-to-Classic transition. The ceramics from Site AZ T:3:52(ASM) indicated a Hohokam occupation during the Sedentary and Classic periods; Tizon Wiped sherds were present as well.

Projectile Point Typology

Of the five projectile points collected from Sites AZ T:3:42(ASM) and AZ T:3:43(ASM), four (Figure 4.1a–d) were diagnostic. The first, a Desert Side-notched point, was recovered from Shelter 1 at AZ T:3:42(ASM). Archaeologists generally consider the Desert Side-notched type to be a Pai and Yavapai cultural diagnostic in western Arizona, with a temporal range of approximately A.D. 1300 to historic times (Pilles 1981). The remaining points were not as strongly diagnostic but probably were associated with the Hohokam occupation. One point and a notched biface in particular (Figures 4.1c, 4.1e) closely resembled pre-Classic Hohokam forms reported from Snaketown (Gladwin et al. 1965:Plates 93d, 94d).

Summary

The prehistoric Hohokam used the project area intermittently over a temporal span beginning in the Colonial period and lasting until the end of the prehistoric sequence. The evidence for Yavapai occupation was somewhat less clear-cut. The radiocarbon dates obtained were equivocal in relation to the associated material culture assemblages. These dates could relate to the late prehistoric use of the sites or to a protohistoric Yavapai or even Apache presence in the area sometime between the sixteenth and eighteenth centuries. The lack of direct association with Yavapai materials and the disturbance in the shelter deposits, however, greatly reduced the utility of these dates.

Evidence for Yavapai use of Site AZ T:3:42(ASM) consisted of a projectile point in Shelter 1, a pot break well away from the shelters, and two radiocarbon dates from Shelter 1 deposits. Again, the evidence suggested that the area may have been used by the Yavapai, but no clear association was evident between the radiocarbon dates, the projectile point, and the pot break.

The evidence indicated that Yavapai groups may have used the area outside of the shelter at Site AZ T:3:52(ASM) as a temporary encampment. The shelter fill yielded no Yavapai material, although a radiocarbon date that suggested use of the shelter during the Protohistoric period came from a sample from the rockshelter. Here again, analysts could make no definite associations among these data.

Finally, Apachean groups may have used the shelter at Site AZ T:3:42(ASM). Four sherds that may have been Rimrock Plain came from the fill of this shelter, and the late radiocarbon date may be associated with this postulated occupation or use. However, as in the Yavapai case, analysts could not demonstrate this association.

Historic Mining Sites

Trash deposits provided reliable chronological evidence for dating Sites AZ T:3:45 and AZ T:3:48 (ASM). In particular, an abundance of temporally sensitive evaporated milk cans indicated occupations prior to and during World War I, from World War I into the Depression, and between 1950 and 1960. Analysts based a possible 1885 ascription on 21 sardine cans of an early type, with some confidence. These occupations appear to be related to fluctuations in demand for ores present in the project area, particularly copper.

SITE FUNCTION

The prehistoric Hieroglyphic Mountains sites studied during data recovery were restricted both in the range of site types present and in material culture. Both prehistoric and protohistoric groups appeared to have used the area almost entirely for exploiting a range of natural plant and animal food resources. The sites lacked evidence of other than temporary shelter, the extant remains consisting of three small rockshelters, a low wall within one of the rockshelters, and, at the two open sites, a circular rock outline, along with insubstantial shelter features. These kinds of shelters were suited to short-term, seasonal occupation by relatively small groups. Group size may have been on the order of one or two families, or perhaps several individuals at most.

Prehistoric material culture was virtually all of a utilitarian nature. With the exception of a single small bird effigy pendant (Figure 4.1) and perhaps a small part of the ceramic collection, none of the recovered artifacts were decorative or ceremonial. Project lithic artifacts were dominated by pounding stones and scrapers, with a fair number of flake and biface knife tools and thinning flakes. Site inhabitants probably used these tools in processing both plant and animal resources. Indirect evidence for use with animal resources lay in the considerable amount of animal bone, including tortoise, rabbit, deer, and several carnivores, recovered from the shelter deposits (Appendix D). Evidence that a number of tools had been used to process plant resources, such as pounding leguminous seeds, was perhaps more circumstantial, although pollen and macrobotanical remains suggested probable cultural use of a number of species. Identified species included plantago, saguaro, dropseed grass, prickly pear, cholla, globemallow, a chenopod or amaranth, and perhaps paloverde (Appendixes B and C).

Excavators recovered ground stone from the five prehistoric sites in moderate amounts. The inhabitants apparently used these implements to grind or crush plant seeds. Since the investigations yielded little evidence of cultigen pollen (one grain of corn pollen) (Appendix B), this processing probably was of wild plant resources. The ground stone assemblage included both flat milling stones and trough metate fragments, although milling stones were more abundant. A number of basin metates and two shallow bedrock grinding surfaces were present as well. In general, the collection showed relatively little formal shaping but did indicate intensive or long-term use of the pieces present.

Excavators recovered no evidence to indicate that occupants of the historic mining sites had made use of local subsistence resources. Their exploitation of the region appeared to be exclusively the extraction of mineral ores.

SETTLEMENT AND SUBSISTENCE

Prehistoric and Protohistoric Occupation

The archaeological literature presents two contrasting models of the use of the upland desert by prehistoric and protohistoric groups. The first model views exploitation of these areas as part of a seasonal-round settlement system; the second considers the area a secondary resource zone (Rice and Dobbins 1981). In the seasonal-round system, a hunter-gatherer economic community moves as a whole in season to a particular resource area. In the second model, specialized work parties seek the same resources from communities based elsewhere. The seasonal-round settlement system can be used to describe the Yavapai presence within the area, while the secondary resource zone model is consistent with the evidence for Hohokam use of this region.

Hohokam Occupation

The predominant Hohokam use of the project area was clearly as a secondary resource zone, although target resources and collection methods may have been generally the same as those of the later Yavapai. Project data suggested an environment structurally or qualitatively similar to that of today throughout the Hohokam and Yavapai occupation periods.

The Hohokam occupation corresponded closely in time with the period of agricultural village settlement of the Agua Fria River and other northern periphery drainages, primarily during the Santa Cruz, Sacaton, and Soho phases. A number of large Hohokam sites are located along the Agua Fria between Lake Pleasant, Calderwood Butte, and the Eastwing and Westwing terminal area. These sites are all within 10 miles of the project area and are the most likely base of prehistoric groups exploiting the project area. From these riverine sites, trips to the project area could have been of short duration, and flexibility in scheduling and group composition may have been considerable.

Analysis of the cultural materials from the project area indicated that the Hohokam exploited a wide range of resources. This interpretation would be consistent with the proximity of permanent villages and the consequent ability to schedule forays to take advantage of resources that ripen during different times of the year.

Yavapai Occupation

Ethnographic studies of the Yavapai indicate that saguaro, paloverde, mesquite, ironwood, deer, tortoise, and rabbit were the most important locally available wild animal food resources (Gifford 1932, 1936). Cactus fruit and bean pods were typically available from mid June into July. Collection parties included both men and women and probably consisted of at least one or more family units. The project area was probably too far from Yavapai base camps to be considered as a gathering locus for late-winter greens or fall-ripening seeds except under conditions of unusual stress.

The evidence from the project area was quite compatible with the ethnographic Yavapai model of small but heterogeneous task groups occupying the area for a period of a few weeks to a year and exploiting specific subsistence resources. Unfortunately for clarity of interpretation, Yavapai material was mixed with earlier Hohokam remains at both shelter sites. The processes of site use, bioturbation, and probable artifact reuse created a difficult and, in some respects, an impoverished record.

Historic Euroamerican Occupation

Exploitation of the historic resources was also as a secondary resource zone, to extend this concept from the pre-industrial to the more complex and energy-intensive modern context. Occupying groups sought very specific resources here, and a specialized segment of society carried out this exploitation. The material support for their work was of outside origin and was largely consumed during the process.

SUMMARY

Gasser (1979) has suggested that Hohokam access to and use of foods from upland secondary resource zones was important in allowing fully sedentary occupation of lowland agricultural sites. The Hieroglyphic Mountains, along with other midrange upland areas in the local region, may at times have played this critical role for prehistoric settlers along the Agua Fria River and adjacent drainages. The need to complement and supplement agricultural and other lowland resources may have determined the level of use of the project area. Prevailing environmental conditions and possible overuse of favored areas near the permanent settlements may have limited such use. Correspondingly, the paloverde-saguaro zone was undoubtedly critical to the stability of the Yavapai adaptation and maintenance of well-established base camps in the upland chaparral zone. Logistical problems related to scheduling and distance from these base camps probably limited Yavapai exploitation of this region.

Historic use of the Hieroglyphic Mountains project area was limited to small-scale mining and stock grazing and the minor transportation routes attendant on these activities. The two mining sites studied here indicated activity beginning as early as the 1880s, circa World War I, in the 1920s, and in the 1950s. Dating of the later components was based on larger artifact collections than were present at the earlier components. It is unfortunate that researchers found neither archival nor informant data pertaining specifically to these sites.

APPENDIXES

APPENDIX A

RADIOCARBON RESULTS

Beta Analytic, Inc.

APPENDIX A

RADIOCARBON RESULTS

SWCA submitted three samples of wood charcoal to Beta Analytic, Inc., of Coral Gables, Florida, for radiocarbon age determinations. Table A.1 presents the results of the analysis, along with tree-ring-corrected dates (Klein et al. 1982).

Table A.1. Radiocarbon Dating Results

Site No. (ASM)	Laboratory No.	Uncorrected Date	Tree-Ring-Calibrated Ranges
AZ T:3:42	27148	320 years B.P. ±60 (A.D. 1570–1690)	A.D. 1422–1678 and A.D. 1484–1684[2]
	27149	300 years B.P. ±50 (A.D. 1600–1700)	A.D. 1430–1660
AZ T:3:52	27150	270 years B.P. ±50 (A.D. 1630–1730)	A.D. 1485–1665 and A.D. 1760–1795[3]

[1]From Klein et al. 1982.
[2]Extrapolated from table entry for 320±50 (A.D. 1425–1655) and 320±100 (A.D. 1410–1800), based on two calibrated ranges of A.D. 1410–1670 and A.D. 1720–1800).
[3]Combination of two calibrated ranges is A.D. 1485–1795.

APPENDIX B

POLLEN ANALYSIS

Suzanne K. Fish

APPENDIX B

POLLEN ANALYSIS

Suzanne K. Fish

The pollen analysis included two samples from Site AZ T:3:41(ASM) and seven from Site AZ T:3:42(ASM). Distributions of pollen types suggested the introduction of several plant resources by prehistoric inhabitants.

METHODS

Laboratory personnel extracted samples by heavy liquid flotation with zinc bromide (density 2.0). Hydrochloric and hydrofluoric acid rinses removed additional extraneous material. As the basis for the percentage calculations of individual types shown in Table B.1, the analyst identified 200 pollen grains from each sample, excluding cultigens, then tabulated cultigen types in addition to this standard sum and quantitatively presented *Zea,* or corn, the only type in this category, as the number of grains encountered during tabulation of the other 200 types. For additional details on these procedures, see Fish (1984). Table B.1 presents the results of the analysis.

ENVIRONMENTAL INDICATIONS

Pollen spectra from AZ T:3:41(ASM) and from both rockshelters at AZ T:3:42(ASM) reflected patterns consistent with current vegetation in the project area. Shrubby and herbaceous plants were the sources of the great majority of pollen present, as is typical of desertscrub communities that also include abundant arborescent species such as leguminous trees and saguaros (Hevly, Mehringer, and Yocum 1965; Schoenwetter and Doerschlag 1971). *Ambrosia*-type pollen was probably contributed by bursage, although canyon ragweeds also might account for minor quantities. The high-spine Compositae category correlates with a number of shrubby plants and herbaceous annuals.

Paloverde (*Cercidium*) pollen came from both sites, but mesquite (*Prosopis*) occurred only in three adjacent levels in Shelter 1 at AZ T:3:42(ASM). These trees do not disperse pollen abundantly, and detection of mesquite in these proveniences may be due to chance. However, it is possible that the presence of this type in Shelter 1 and only there indicates occupation during a period when mesquites were more accessible about the spring or along a wash floodplain. Differential resource use could also account for this localization of mesquite pollen. Other desert taxa found at both sites included creosotebush (*Larrea*) and cholla (*Cylindropuntia*). Only the larger group of samples from AZ T:3:42(ASM) yielded prickly pear (*Platyopuntia*) and *Cereus*-type pollen (including similar types produced by saguaro, hedgehog, and related cacti).

The quantitatively variable representation of Cheno-am pollen (chenopods and amaranths) among the samples almost surely denotes intensity of cultural disturbance. Herbaceous chenopods and amaranths colonize the enriched and disturbed environs of human residence and activity, elevating proportions of this type above natural background levels contributed by such species as saltbush (*Atriplex*). Elevated frequencies may also result from introduction of greens or seeds as resources. Other pollen types that are associated with cultural disturbance, particularly with agricultural activity (Fish 1985), were relatively

Table B.1. Pollen Types as Percentage of 200-grain Count per Sample

Pollen Type	AZ T:3:41(ASM)		AZ T:3:42(ASM)						
	F1	F7	Shelter 1				Shelter 2		
	*0**	*10*	*15***	*10*	*25*	*40*	*15*	*30*	*55*
Ambrosia[++]	29.0	20.5	19.5	32.0	33.0	29.5	41.5	27.0	46.0
Boerhaavia[++]	2.5	1.0		1.0	1.5	+		0.5	
Cercidium	0.5		0.5		1.0				
Cereus[++]				0.5				+	
Cheno-am	19.0	12.5	54.5	19.5	26.5	8.0	11.5	29.0[a]	12.5
Cruciferae	0.5					1.5			
Cylindropuntia		2.5		3.5	5.0[a]			0.5	
Ephedra	3.0	1.5	0.5		2.5	2.5	0.5	4.0	
Eriogonum	9.0	3.5	0.5	4.5	3.0	7.5	0.5	2.5	
Euphorbia[++]	0.5			1.5		2.0	1.0		0.5
Gramineae	4.5	17.5[a]	6.0	8.0[a]	2.0	9.5	5.5	5.0	3.5
High-spine Compositae	20.5	28.0	10.0	24.0	9.5	19.0	25.5	22.0	31.5
Juniperus	0.5	2.5	0.5	1.0	2.0		3.0	1.5	
Larrea	0.5					1.0	1.0		
cf. Leguminosae		0.5	3.0		0.5			0.5	
Pinus	6.0	2.5	3.0	1.5	4.5	9.5	7.5	2.0	4.0
Platyopuntia					1.0			0.5	
Prosopis				0.5	1.0	4.0			
Quercus	+	1.0			2.0		0.5		0.5
Sphaeralcea		1.5	0.5		1.0			3.0[a]	
Zea[2]							1.0		
Other	1.0	0.5		0.5	0.5	1.0		1.0	
Indeterminate	3.0	4.5	1.5	2.0	3.5	5.0	2.0	0.5	1.5

*cm below ground surface **ash and charcoal cluster
[a]aggregate of six or more pollen grains
+observation made after completion of 200-grain count ++pollen type

low in frequency in the samples. Minor percentages of spiderling (*Boerhaavia)* and globemallow (*Sphaeralcea*) in the assemblage fell within a lower range than has been found at more substantial habitation sites in the region (e.g., Bohrer 1984). Wild buckwheat (*Eriogonum*), another plant that responds to disturbance, was somewhat more abundant.

SITE POLLEN RECORDS

AZ T:3:41(ASM)

The two samples from Site AZ T:3:41(ASM) were similar in overall distributions. Both Cheno-am and wild buckwheat pollen were somewhat higher at Feature 1, as might be expected for weedy plants responding to concentrated cultural disturbance in the vicinity of a structure. However, Cheno-am values did not attain the high levels encountered at many long-term habitation sites in Sonoran Desert environments, and it is probable that the occupation of Feature 1 was of limited duration.

Feature 7 yielded the site's only economic indications, a high frequency of grass (*Gramineae*) pollen from unidentified species associated with pollen aggregates. The small amounts of cholla pollen were also probably economic in origin, since the amounts found would be in the upper range for spectra from natural communities. Cholla buds are a likely source.

AZ T:3:42(ASM)

Investigators took samples from two rockshelters at AZ T:3:42(ASM), a site encompassing a small spring. Shelter 2, with Hohokam occupations, showed evidence of substantial rodent disturbance. The samples from Level 6 (50–60 cm below ground surface) produced no clear evidence for resource use. Level 2 (10–20 cm below ground surface) produced the only cultigen pollen in the present analysis, a single grain of corn pollen. Such a trace amount could have been introduced by processed supplies brought to the site from elsewhere. Relatively high frequencies and aggregates of chenopods or amaranths indicated their use at the shelter. Globemallow aggregates suggested an additional resource. The Navajo used globemallow seeds as food (Elmore 1944), and many Southwestern groups used the plants medicinally (Curtin 1984; Gallagher 1977).

Hohokam and possibly Yavapai groups had occupied Shelter 1. One sample was associated with an ash and charcoal cluster, and the remainder constituted a stratigraphic series from the south-wall excavation profile. The cluster association, from 15 cm below ground surface, yielded an unusually high frequency of Cheno-am pollen. Chenopods and amaranths may have been stored or cooked in this shelter.

The uppermost sample in the stratigraphic series, from a pebbly stratum with some artifacts, contained cholla pollen in a probably economic concentration. *Cereus*-type pollen is produced by economically important saguaro, hedgehog, and related cactus species; however, the single grain in the sample may represent a natural background frequency. Pollen aggregates contributing to a moderate frequency of grass pollen represented the third possible economic evidence in this level; either subsistence or craft uses could be involved.

In the ashy-gray stratum beneath the pebbly layer, cholla pollen was again present, as was prickly pear pollen. Pollen aggregates as well as an overall high value for cholla pollen supported an economic interpretation of its presence. Because prickly pear pollen is not dispersed widely beyond the plant, its presence here was also a likely cultural indication. The project radiocarbon dates leave open the possibility that the two uppermost levels were post-contact in age. Wild resources, particularly cacti, were most abundant.

A sample from the Shelter 1 roof-fall level produced no evidence for resource use, with the possible exception of mesquite. This stratum contained the highest frequency of mesquite pollen and was the lowermost among three consecutive samples containing this pollen type. The stratigraphic pattern may have reflected an interval during which mesquite trees grew abundantly below the rockshelter. Cheno-am values in the roof-fall level were the lowest in the series, denoting a relative minimum of cultural impact on vegetation in the vicinity. The lowermost sample had similarly low Cheno-am frequencies and no economic indications.

CONCLUSIONS

The inhabitants of both AZ T:3:41(ASM) and AZ T:3:42(ASM) appeared to have depended primarily on wild resources, collecting cacti, chenopods and amaranths, and grasses. Cholla buds would have been gathered in the spring, perhaps in April, and prickly pear fruits later in the summer. Lacking identifications to the species level, the analyst could not further narrow probable seasonal ranges for exploitation of cacti. Only Shelter 2 at AZ T:3:42(ASM) yielded any evidence of cultigens. The trace amount of corn pollen recovered may well represent importation rather than local production.

APPENDIX C

MACROBOTANICAL ANALYSIS

Lisa W. Huckell

APPENDIX C

MACROBOTANICAL ANALYSIS

Lisa W. Huckell

The 14 flotation and 2 macrofossil samples submitted for analysis were from three project sites. Two were small, shallow rockshelters (AZ T:3:42[ASM] and AZ T:3:52[ASM]), and the third was an open site with surface features (AZ T:3:41[ASM]). The samples—seven flotation samples and two macrofossil lots—consisted almost exclusively of noncarbonized plant and animal materials that offered little additional information on aboriginal subsistence in the Hieroglyphic Mountains area.

METHODS

Laboratory personnel processed all of the flotation samples using the method developed by Bohrer and Adams (1977). They passed completely dry flotation residues through a graduated geological screen series that divided the material into five size classes:

(a) > 4.75 mm
(b) 2.00–4.75 mm
(c) 1.00–2.00 mm
(d) 0.50–1.00 mm
(e) < 0.50 mm

This procedure facilitates efficiency and accuracy in sorting and is useful when the analysis requires subsampling of large quantities of material.

The analyst sorted the samples with a binocular stereozoom microscope with a magnification range of 7–30X and identified and counted carbonized plant remains, which are more likely than unburned remains to be aboriginal rather than present through natural means, as well as unburned plant remains and any small bones, teeth, and terrestrial molluscs. The analyst then used this information, along with observations on the quantities of insect parts and fecal pellets present, to assess the degree of disturbance sustained by the sampled site areas.

The analysis included all of the three largest-class fractions of each sample; depending on the volume and composition of a particular fraction, either all or subsamples of size class (d); and subsamples of size class (e). Sample totals for the subsampled size classes were estimated.

The analyst retrieved all complete and fragmentary items with diagnostic or distinctive features, identified them to the most specific taxonomic level possible, and placed them in protective gelatin capsules. Eighty of the recovered specimens were unidentifiable. These unknowns ranged from tiny endosperm and seed-coat fragments to partial seeds and embryos that had sustained considerable damage.

The analyst based identifications on Martin and Barkley 1973, Parker 1972, and modern seed samples in her comparative collection. The taxonomy employed follows Kearney and Peebles 1964.

RESULTS

Analysis began with samples from one of the rockshelters, Site AZ T:3:52(ASM). That considerable mixing had taken place in the shelter fill quickly became apparent. Samples from all three excavation levels were virtually identical in overall composition, displaying extensive inventories of modern seed taxa, modest amounts of wood charcoal, large quantities of fecal pellets, and significant numbers of insect (especially ant) exoskeletal fragments, small bones, and mollusc shells. With two possible exceptions, the remains did not include carbonized seeds. Examination of a sample from the lowest level in each of the two shelters at Site AZ T:3:42(ASM) to see whether this pattern was characteristic of the other shelters indicated that the overall picture was much the same, with the addition of some carbonized items. Excavation records also indicated considerable downward mixing in both shelters and chewed bits of plastic distributed through all fill levels in Shelter 2. Shelter 2 also contained a large nest constructed by woodrats. The seed collecting and burrowing propensities of these rodents are well known. Given the meager quantity of carbonized material present and the equivocal nature of the fill, the analyst did not study additional samples from these two sites.

Within Site AZ T:3:41(ASM), the two loci sampled for flotation analysis were a trench placed through Feature 1 (a long rock cluster that may have represented a windbreak) and Feature 7 (a fire pit containing 13 cm of ashy fill). The sample from Feature 1 contained no carbonized plant remains whatsoever, but it did yield eight modern seed types whose presence was most likely the result of insect or rodent activity. The second sample produced seven carbonized seed types, along with seven modern types and a very high estimated fecal pellet count.

Two lots of uncarbonized seeds examined were from AZ T:3:52(ASM), Unit A, 10–20 cm below ground surface, and Shelter 2 at AZ T:3:42(ASM), Unit C, 5 cm below ground surface. The Unit A lot consisted of six seeds of foothill paloverde (*Cercidium microphyllum* [Torr.] Rose and Johnson). The second macrofossil sample proved to be a single seed of *C. microphyllum*. None of the seeds showed evidence of gnawing or other modification.

Table C.1 summarizes the results of the analysis, for the sake of brevity and relevance showing only carbonized specimens. The analyst made no adjustment for fragmentary specimens, counting all identified items equally. The entries in the table indicate both the actual number of an item counted and the estimated number in the sample (in parentheses).

As Table C.1 shows, three samples yielded identifiable carbonized plant remains. Of the nine taxa represented, five are known to have economic significance. Southwestern Indian groups have used *Plantago* seeds for food and medicine (Curtin 1984:96-97; Felger and Moser 1985:354; Weber and Seaman 1985:242). These seeds have also been recovered from prehistoric Hohokam sites (Gasser 1981:Table 1). The consumption of cactus fruits and their seeds by both prehistoric and historic Native American groups has been extensively documented (Castetter 1935; Felger and Moser 1985:245-273; Fontana 1980; Gasser 1981). All of the genera recovered from the project sites have been utilized for food to some degree, although it was the seasonally abundant saguaro fruit that was, and still is, most frequently and extensively exploited. Wild grasses were also important dietary components in the Southwest (Doebley 1984).

Sporobolus is one of several genera known to have been collected for food. Gasser (1981:225) reported that it has also been recovered from prehistoric sites. Little can be said of the unidentified taxa. The badly damaged Compositae achenes bore some resemblance to brittle bush (*Encilia farinosa* Gray),

Table C.1. Distribution of Carbonized Remains from Macrobotanical Samples

Taxon	AZ T:3:41(ASM)		AZ T:3:42(ASM)		AZ T:3:52(ASM)		
	Feature 1	Feature 7	Shelter 1	Shelter 2	Shelter		
		*5–10 cmbs**	*55–65 cmbs*	*60–70 cmbs*	*0–10 cmbs*	*10–15 cmbs*	*25–28 cmbs*
Botanical Remains							
Seeds							
Carnegiea gigantea (saguaro)		4		6			
Echinocereus sp. (hedgehog cactus)		1		1			
Ferocactus sp. (barrel cactus)		2					
Leguminosae (legumes)		70(118)**					
species 1				1			
species 2							
Plantago sp. (plantain)		7(23)					
Caryopses							
Gramineae (grasses)		4(20)					
Sporobolus sp. (dropseed)			1(10)				
Achenes							
cf. Compositae (sunflower-type)		2					
Unknowns		58(64)	1(10)	21(26)	2(12)		
Total Botanical Remains		**148(254)**	**2(20)**	**29(34)**	**2(12)**		
Nonbotanical Remains							
Bones/Teeth		2	4(8)	66(76)	1	6	13
Snails		9	10(18)	129(154)	1(6)	12(25)	30(45)

*cm below surface **Numbers in parentheses represent estimated size of sample.

uncarbonized achenes of which were in some of the flotation residues. The two leguminous species represented included 70 specimens of a tiny globose seed with average dimensions of 1.4 × 1.1 × 1.1 mm and a single incomplete specimen of a small, kidney-shaped seed that measured 1.3 × 1.7 x 0.6 mm.

DISCUSSION

The difficulty in distinguishing between culturally and naturally introduced plant parts made assessment of the plant remains from the Hieroglyphic Mountains sites difficult. This topic has been the subject of considerable discussion (Keepaz 1977; Minnis 1981; Spector 1970), with the consensus that carbonization, as a reflection of cultural activity, is the best criterion for distinguishing economic plant use, especially for open-site assemblages. The situation for more protected environments such as caves and shelters, however, is not so simple to resolve. Perishable artifacts and foodstuffs that would quickly disappear in an open context often remain essentially intact when left in an environment that reduces moisture, hostile soil chemistry, predators, fungi, and other destructive forces. The drawback to this favorable condition is the confusion resulting from contamination. Shelters are also preferred habitation sites for birds, mammals, reptiles, and insects. In particular, granivorous species of rodents and insects are capable of introducing large quantities of seeds and associated plant materials into shelter fills from distances up to 50 m away (Betancourt and Davis 1984:56). Humans also exploited many of the seed species collected by animals and insects. In the absence of evidence for deliberate human modification (cut marks, singeing or burning, and so forth), no reliable means exist for discriminating between the two modes of introduction. The obvious major exception would be the presence of cultigens, which are exclusively tied to human activity.

Given the uncertain origins of the plant remains, the small quantities of carbonized macrofossils recovered, the relatively shallow fill of the shelters, and the extensive bioturbation of the shelter deposits, the flotation results from the Hieroglyphic Mountains sites must be considered highly equivocal. The moderate quantities of charcoal found in the samples were probably generated by fires built within or immediately in front of the shelters. However, the lack of association with definable features or securely dated strata, coupled with the mixing that has taken place, minimized the possibility of deriving useful information regarding site occupation from the charcoal samples. Conceivably, such fires could also be indirectly responsible for the few carbonized items retrieved from the shelter fills, as the close proximity of rodent- or insect-transported seeds to the fire could have resulted in inadvertent charring. This process could account for the burned seeds recovered from the hearth at AZ T:3:41(ASM), that is, the burning of the seeds could have been the accidental byproduct of the placement of the feature on or adjacent to a cache of seeds. Alternatively, rodents or insects could have concealed the seeds under the hearth rocks between uses of the feature. Although most of the seed taxa represented at the feature are known to have been used culturally and could represent food preparation by site occupants, the possibility that they were accidental inclusions in the hearth fill must be considered equally likely.

APPENDIX D

FAUNAL ANALYSIS

Linda J. Pierce

APPENDIX D

FAUNAL ANALYSIS

Linda J. Pierce

METHODS

Three rockshelters excavated during the Hieroglyphic Mountains project yielded faunal remains. Excavation of the shelter at Site AZ T:3:52(ASM) produced a small sample of 56 bones and bone fragments. At AZ T:3:42(ASM), Shelter 1 yielded 386 bones and Shelter 2 produced 466 bones. Staff of the Zooarchaeology Laboratory of the Arizona State Museum (ASM) cleaned, identified, and analyzed all of the bone.

To make identifications, the analyst used the Western Archeological Conservation Center comparative collection housed at ASM and curated by Professor S. J. Olsen. The goal was to make identifications to the species level, but in some instances only a genus, family, or order level identification was possible due to the fragmented nature of the bone or the nonspecific nature of many bone features. The analyst separated the bones into general animal size categories when only a class identification (e.g., Mammalia) was possible. All identifications are the responsibility of the analyst.

The quantitative measures used in this analysis are the NISP (number of identifiable specimens) and the MNI (minimum number of individuals). The NISP is simply the number of bones and fragments identified in a specific taxonomic category. The MNI is a measure of the minimum number of animals of a given taxon needed to account for all the bones recovered, calculated by determining the most abundant element from a given taxon.

RESULTS

AZ T:3:42(ASM)

Determining whether animal remains in an archaeological site are natural or cultural can be difficult. The presence of burning or other cultural modification is often used as a criterion. Among the fauna identified from the two shelters at AZ T:3:42(ASM) (Tables D.1 and D.2), the snake, toad, and bird bones were probably intrusive. None were burned, and the small quantities recovered suggested that they occurred naturally. All of these animals were residents of the site area.

Little evidence suggested cultural use of the rodent bone recovered, although the possibility that site inhabitants used the woodrat (*Neotoma* sp.), which dominated the rodent assemblage, as food cannot be ruled out. The woodrat is a large rodent that both burrows and builds nests above ground. The large woodrat nest seen at Shelter 2 is clear evidence that these rodents lived in the immediate area of the site. They would have been easily accessible to the occupants of the shelters, and six of the woodrat bones were burned.

Mandibles dominated the woodrat assemblage, the result not of cultural activities but of preservation and recovery. One of the most durable bones of a rodent skeleton, due to its size and shape the mandible is more likely to be caught and recovered from a 1/4-inch screen than other bone from animals of this size.

Table D.1. Faunal Remains, AZ T:3:42(ASM), Shelter 1

Taxon	**NISP**	**Number Burned**	**Percent Burned**	**MNI**
Artiodactyla (deer, antelope)	13	8	61.5	-
Carnivora (carnivore)	1	0	0.0	1
Gopherus agassizi (desert tortoise)	1	1	100.0	1
Lepus californicus (black-tailed jackrabbit	18	3	16.7	2
Leporidae (rabbit, hare)	1	1	100.0	1
Neotoma sp. (woodrat)	70	4	5.7	21
Odocoileus hemionus (mule deer)	1	0	0.0	1
Odocoileus sp. (deer, mule or white-tail)	4	1	25.0	1
Perognathus sp. (pocket mouse)	1	0	0.0	1
Peromyscus sp. or *Reithrodontomys* sp. (New World mouse)	2	0	0.0	1
Phasianidae (quail)	1	0	0.0	1
Procyon lotor (raccoon)	2	2	100.0	1
Rodentia (rodent)	3	1	33.3	1
Sylvilagus sp. (cottontail rabbit)	25	2	8.0	2
Taxidea taxus (badger)	1	0	0.0	1
Small mammal (rabbit-sized)	27	7	25.9	-
Medium mammal (coyote-sized)	1	0	0.0	-
Medium-large mammal (coyote- to deer-sized)	9	8	88.9	-
Large mammal (deer-sized)	196	80	40.8	-
Mammal, size unknown	9	2	22.2	-
Total	**386**	**120**	**31.1**	**36**

Table D.2. Faunal Remains, AZ T:3:42(ASM), Shelter 2

Taxon	**NISP**	**Number Burned**	**Percent Burned**	**MNI**
Artiodactyla (deer, antelope)	28	13	46.4	-
Aves (bird)	1	0	0.0	1
Bufo sp. (toad)	6	0	0.0	1
Canis sp. (coyote, dog)	3	2	66.7	2
Carnivora (carnivore)	2	0	0.0	1
Felis rufus (bobcat)	5	4	80.0	1
Gopherus agassizi (desert tortoise)				
Leporidae (rabbit, hare)	1	0	0.0	-
Lepus californicus (black-tailed jackrabbit)	28	5	17.9	3
Neotoma sp. (woodrat)	63	2	3.2	16
Odocoileus hemionus (mule deer)	8	2	25.0	1
Ovis canadensis (bighorn sheep)	1	1	100.0	1
Phasianidae (quail)	1	0	0.0	1
Rodentia (rodent)	14	5	35.7	2
Snake	5	0	0.0	1
Sylvilagus sp. (cottontail rabbit)	39	3	7.7	5
Tayassu tajacu (collared peccary)	1	0	0.0	-
Zenaidura macroura (mourning dove)	2	0	0.0	1
Small mammal (rabbit-sized)	39	9	23.1	-
Small-medium mammal (rabbit- to coyote-sized)	2	1	50.0	-
Medium mammal (coyote-sized)	1	1	100.0	-
Medium-large mammal (coyote- to deer-sized)	40	17	42.5	-
Large mammal (deer-sized)	95	28	29.5	-
Mammal, size unknown	57	3	5.3	-
Total	**446**	**108**	**23.2**	**39**

Twenty-four *Gopherus agassizi* remains, half of them burned, were good evidence for cultural use of the desert tortoise at Shelter 2 at AZ T:3:42(ASM). These specimens included both carapace pieces and limb bones. The quantity recovered and the amount of burned bone suggest that the tortoise was a food source. None of the carapace pieces showed evidence of working.

Bones of leporids and large artiodactyls were the most numerous remains recovered from the two shelters. These animals are the expected, major faunal protein food sources in the prehistoric southwestern United States. Few of the artiodactyl bones were identifiable to the genus or species level, but the assemblages included a large number of unidentifiable bone fragments from mammals of this size. The fragmented nature of the large mammal bones suggested cultural processing for soups or marrow extraction.

One interesting aspect of this assemblage was the diversity of carnivore bones, including identifiable remains of coyote or dog, raccoon, badger, and bobcat. This is an unusual sample for an assemblage of this size, and many of these bones were burned.

The faunal assemblage suggested that these shelters were used by hunting groups. The natural spring located near the shelters would have attracted many of the animals found in the collection, probably the reason carnivores were so well represented. None of the animals recovered were unusual species that would not be expected in the area. The presence of water would, perhaps, have given human hunters an advantage in exploiting the various species recovered.

AZ T:3:52(ASM)

The faunal collection from this site was very small (Table D.3). *Neotoma* sp. bones made up almost half of the assemblage. Determining whether rodent bones from archaeological sites are natural or cultural remains is notoriously difficult because most rodents are burrowers. Burned elements from the peripheral skeleton of rodents can be an indicator of cultural deposition (Szuter 1984:156), but none of the rodent elements recovered from AZ T:3:52(ASM) were burned.

Although woodrats build houses above the ground, they nest and burrow below ground level. Excavators observed live woodrats in the shelter during data recovery, and the woodrat bones recovered from the excavation most likely represented post-occupational intrusion.

The uppermost levels of the shelter yielded three carapace pieces from *Gopherus agassizi,* which could have been a food source. None of these elements were burned, however, and since the desert tortoise burrows, the pieces recovered may have been intrusive. The analyst could not specifically identify any deer or antelope bones, but the assemblage did include six fragments from deer-sized long bones, one of them burned. As with the remains from AZ T:3:42(ASM), the fragmented nature of these bones suggested cultural processing, perhaps for soups or for marrow extraction.

The assemblage from AZ T:3:52(ASM) included bones from both cottontail rabbits (*Sylvilagus* sp.) and jackrabbits (*Lepus californicus*), as do the majority of archaeological sites in the Southwest. These animals were standard and reliable prehistoric food sources.

Table D.3. Faunal Remains, AZ T:3:52(ASM)

Taxon	NISP	Number Burned	Percent Burned	MNI
Canis sp. (coyote or dog	1			1
Gopherus agassizi (desert tortoise)	3			1
Lepus californicus (black-tailed jackrabbit)	2			1
Neotoma sp. (woodrat)	27			9
Rodentia (rodent)	2			1
Sylvilagus sp. (cottontail rabbit)	8			2
Small Mammal (rabbit-sized)	5			
Medium Mammal (coyote-sized)	1	1	100.0	
Large Mammal (deer-sized)	6	1	16.7	
Mammal (size unknown)	1			
Total	**56**	**2**	**3.6**	**15**

The single bone from a coyote or dog (*Canis* sp.) was identified only to genus because faunal analysts cannot distinguish between coyotes and similar-sized dogs using post-cranial skeletal elements. This element was a right ulna, slightly worked along one long edge. Although broken, it appeared to have been an awl fragment.

Summary

Few conclusions can be drawn from a faunal sample of this size. In general, the animals represented would be expected in this area. The awl fragment was the only bone tool recovered from the project area.

REFERENCES

Abbott, David R.

1988 Form, Function, Technology, and Style in Hohokam Ceramics. In *The 1982-1984 Excavations at Las Colinas: Material Culture*, by David R. Abbott, Kim E. Beckwith, Patricia L. Crown, R. Thomas Euler, David A. Gregory, J. Ronald London, Marilyn B. Saul, Larry A. Schwalbe, Mary Bernard-Shaw, Christine R. Szuter, and Arthur W. Vokes, pp. 73-197. Arizona State Museum Archaeological Series No. 163, Vol. 4. The University of Arizona, Tucson.

Antieau, John M., and Renee C. Pepoy

1981 Material Culture: Pottery. In *The Palo Verde Archaeological Investigations, Hohokam Settlement at the Confluence: Excavations Along the Palo Verde Pipeline*, edited by John M. Antieau, pp. 146-180. Museum of Northern Arizona Research Papers No. 20. Flagstaff.

Arizona State Bureau of Mines

1961 *Gold Placers and Placering in Arizona*. Arizona State Bureau of Mines Bulletin No. 168. University of Arizona Press, Tucson.

Ayres, James E.

1967 A Prehistoric Farm Site near Cave Creek, Arizona. *The Kiva* 32(3):106-111.

Bernard-Shaw, Mary

1984 Artifacts. In *Hohokam Archaeology along the Salt-Gila Aqueduct, Central Arizona Project: Prehistoric Occupation of the Queen Creek Delta*, edited by Lynn S. Teague and Patricia L. Crown, pp. 447-481. Arizona State Museum Archaeological Series No. 150, Vol. 4. The University of Arizona, Tucson.

Betancourt, Julio L., and Owen K. Davis

1984 Packrat Middens from Canyon de Chelly, Northeastern Arizona: Paleoecological and Archaeological Implications. *Quaternary Research* 21:56-64.

Bohrer, Vorsila L.

1984 Domesticated and Wild Crops in the CAEP Study Area. In *Prehistoric Cultural Development in Central Arizona: Archaeology of the Upper New River Region*, edited by George J. Gumerman and Patricia M. Spoerl, pp. 183-259. Southern Illinois University Center for Archaeological Investigations Occasional Paper No. 5. Carbondale.

Bohrer, Vorsila L., and Karen R. Adams

1977 *Ethnobotanical Techniques and Approaches at Salmon Ruin, New Mexico*. Eastern New Mexico University Contributions in Anthropology No. 8, Vol. 1. Portales.

Bordaz, Jacques

1970 *Tools of the Old and New Stone Age*. Natural History Press, Garden City.

Bordes, Francois

1969 Reflections on Typology and Techniques in the Paleolithic. *Arctic Anthropology* 6(1):1-21.

Brown, David E., Neil B. Carmony, and R. M. Turner
1979 *Drainage Map of Arizona Showing Perennial Streams and Some Important Wetlands*. 2nd ed. Arizona Game and Fish Department, Phoenix.

Busch, Jane
1981 An Introduction to the Tin Can. *Historical Archaeology* 15(1):95-104.

Castetter, Edward F.
1935 *Ethnobiological Studies in the American Southwest I: Uncultivated Native Plants Used as Sources of Food*. University of New Mexico Bulletin No. 266, Biological Series No. 4. Albuquerque.

Colton, Harold S.
1941 *Winona and Ridge Ruin, Part II: Notes on the Technology and Taxonomy of the Pottery*. Museum of Northern Arizona Bulletin No. 19. Flagstaff.

Corbusier, William F.
1886 The Apache-Yumas and Apache-Mojaves. *The American Antiquarian and Oriental Journal* 8(5):276-284.

Cordell, Linda S.
1984 *Prehistory of the Southwest*. Academic Press, Orlando.

Crabtree, Don E.
1972 *An Introduction to Flintworking, Part 1: An Introduction to the Technology of Stone Tools*. Occasional Papers of the Idaho State University No. 28. Pocatello.

Crown, Patricia L.
1981 Analysis of the Las Colinas Ceramics. In *The 1968 Excavations at Mound 8, Las Colinas Ruins Group, Phoenix, Arizona*, edited and assembled by Laurens C. Hammack and Alan P. Sullivan, pp 87-169. Arizona State Museum Archaeological Series No. 154. The University of Arizona, Tucson.

Crown, Patricia L., and Earl W. Sires
1984 The Hohokam Chronology and Salt-Gila Aqueduct Project Research. In *Hohokam Archaeology along the Salt-Gila Aqueduct, Central Arizona Project: Synthesis and Conclusions*, edited by Lynn S. Teague and Patricia L. Crown, pp. 73-85. Arizona State Museum Archaeological Series No. 150, Vol. 9. The University of Arizona, Tucson.

Curtin, L. S. M.
1984 *By the Prophet of the Earth: Ethnobotany of the Pima*. University of Arizona Press, Tucson.

Doebley, John F.
1984 "Seeds" of Wild Grasses: A Major Food of Southwestern Indians. *Economic Botany* 38(1):52-64.

Dosh, Steven G.
1989 *Archaeology along Picacho Wash, Hieroglyphic Mountains, Northern Maricopa County, Arizona*. Project No. R89-35-01. Northland Research, Inc., Flagstaff.

Dove, Donald E.
1970 *A Site Survey along the Lower Agua Fria River, Arizona*. The Arizona Archaeologist No. 5. Arizona Archaeological and Historical Society, Phoenix.

Doyel, David E.
1984 Sedentary Period Hohokam Paleo-economy in the New River Drainage, Central Arizona. In *Prehistoric Agricultural Strategies in the Southwest*, edited by Suzanne K. Fish and Paul R. Fish, pp. 35-52. Arizona State University Anthropological Research Papers No. 33. Tempe.

Doyel, David E., and Mark D. Elson
1985 Ceramic Analysis. In *Hohokam Settlement and Economic Systems in the Central New River Drainage, Arizona*, edited by David E. Doyel and Mark D. Elson, pp. 437-519. Soil Systems Publications in Archaeology No. 4. Phoenix.

Dunning, Charles H.
1966 *Rock to Riches: The Story of American Mining, Past, Present, and Future, as Reflected in the Colorful History of Mining in Arizona, the Nation's Greatest Bonanza*. Hicks, Pasadena.

Elmore, F. H.
1944 *Ethnobotany of the Navajo*. School of American Research Monographs No. 8. Albuquerque.

Euler, Robert C., and Henry F. Dobyns
1958 Tizon Brown Ware. In *Pottery Types of the Southwest*, edited by Harold S. Colton. Museum of Northern Arizona Ceramic Series No. 3D. Flagstaff.

Felger, Richard S., and Mary Beck Moser
1985 *People of the Desert and Sea: Ethnobotany of the Seri Indians*. University of Arizona Press, Tucson.

Ferg, Alan
1977 *Archaeological Survey of the Westwing to Deer Valley Transmission Line, Maricopa County*. Arizona State Museum Archaeological Series No. 111. The University of Arizona, Tucson.

Fish, Suzanne K.
1984 Salt-Gila Pollen Analysis. In *Hohokam Archaeology along the Salt-Gila Aqueduct, Central Arizona Project: Environment and Subsistence*, edited by Lynn S. Teague and Patricia R. Crown, pp. 9-15. Arizona State Museum Archaeology Series No. 150, Vol. 7. The University of Arizona, Tucson.

1985 Prehistoric Disturbance Floras of the Lower Sonoran Desert and their Implications. In *Late Quaternary Vegetation and Climates of the American Southwest*, edited by B. Jacobs, P. Fall, and O. Davis. American Association of Stratigraphic Palynologists Contribution Series No. 16. Houston.

Fontana, Bernard L.
1980 Ethnobotany of the Saguaro, an Annotated Bibliography. *Desert Plants* 2(1):63-78.

Gallagher, Marsha
1977 *Contemporary Ethnobotany among the Apache of the Clarkdale, Arizona Area, Coconino and Prescott National Forests*. USDA Forest Service Southwest Region Archaeological Report No. 14. Albuquerque.

Gasser, Robert E.
1979 Seeds, Seasons, and Ecosystems: Sedentary Hohokam Groups in the Papagueria. *The Kiva* 44:101-111.

1980 Exchange and the Hohokam Archaeological Record. In *Current Issues in Hohokam Prehistory*, edited by David E. Doyel and Fred Plog, pp. 72-77. Arizona State University Anthropological Research Papers No. 23. Tempe.

1981 Hohokam Use of Desert Plant Foods. *Desert Plants* 3(4):216-234.

Gifford, E. W.
1932 *The Southeastern Yavapai*. University of California Publications in American Archaeology and Ethnology No. 29, Vol. 3. Berkeley.

1936 *Northeastern and Western Yavapai*. University of California Publications in American Archaeology and Ethnology No. 34, Vol. 4. Berkeley.

Gillio, David, Frances Levine, and Douglas Scott
1980 *Some Common Artifacts Found at Historical Sites*. USDA Forest Service Southwest Region Cultural Resource Report No. 31. Albuquerque.

Gladwin, Harold W., Emil W. Haury, E. B. Sayles, and Nora Gladwin
1965 *Excavations at Snaketown: Material Culture*. Reprinted. University of Arizona Press, Tucson. Originally published 1938, Medallion Papers No. 25, Gila Pueblo, Globe, Arizona.

Granger, Byrd Howell
1983 *Arizona's Names (X Marks the Spot)*. Falconer, Tucson.

Green, Margerie
1986 *Settlement, Subsistence, and Specialization in the Northern Periphery: Research Design for Mitigative Data Recovery at Sites in the New Waddell Dam Borrow Areas*. Archaeological Consulting Services Cultural Resources Report No. 40. Tempe.

Green, Margerie (editor)
1989 *Settlement, Subsistence, and Specialization in the Northern Periphery: The Waddell Project*. 2 vols. Archaeological Consulting Services Cultural Resources Report No. 65. Tempe.

Green, Margerie, and Richard W. Effland, Jr.
1985 *A Cultural Resource Assessment of the Proposed Agua Fria Borrow Area and Waddell Canal.* Archaeological Consulting Services Cultural Resources Report No. 32. Tempe.

Greenwald, David H.
1988 *Investigations of the Baccharis Site and Extension Arizona Canal: Historic and Prehistoric Land Use Patterns in the Northern Salt River Valley.* Museum of Northern Arizona Research Paper No. 40. Flagstaff.

Greenwald, David H., and Donald R. Keller
1988a Archaeological Inventory Survey of the Hieroglyphic Mountains Tract Federal Land Exchange, Maricopa County, Arizona, with addendum by David A. Gregory. Ms. on file, SWCA, Inc., Environmental Consultants, Flagstaff.

1988b Proposal for Archaeological Investigations at Six Sites in the Hieroglyphic Mountains Tract. Ms. on file, SWCA, Inc., Environmental Consultants, Flagstaff.

Gumerman, George J., and Patricia M. Spoerl
1980 The Hohokam and the Northern Periphery. In *Current Issues in Hohokam Prehistory*, edited by David Doyel and Fred Plog, pp. 134-150. Arizona State University Anthropological Research Papers No. 23. Tempe.

Gumerman, George J., Carol S. Weed, and John S. Hanson
1976 *Adaptive Strategies in a Biological and Cultural Transition Zone: The Central Arizona Ecotone Project, an Interim Report.* Southern Illinois University Museum Studies No. 6. Carbondale.

Haskett, Bert
1935 Early History of the Cattle Industry in Arizona. *Arizona Historical Review* 6:3-42.

Haury, Emil W.
1945 *The Excavations of Los Muertos and Neighboring Ruins in the Salt River Valley, Southern Arizona.* Papers of the Peabody Museum of American Archaeology and Ethnology No. 24, Vol. 1. Harvard University, Cambridge, Massachusetts.

1976 *The Hohokam: Desert Farmers and Craftsmen.* University of Arizona Press, Tucson.

Henderson, T. Kathleen, and James B. Rodgers
1979 *Archaeological Investigations in the Cave Creek Area, Maricopa County, South-Central Arizona.* Arizona State University Anthropological Research Papers No. 17. Tempe.

Hevly, Richard, P. J. Mehringer, and H. G. Yocum
1965 Studies of the Modern Pollen Rain in the Sonoran Desert. *Journal of the Arizona Academy of Sciences* 3:123-135.

Hoffman, Teresa L., and David E. Doyel
1985 Ground Stone Tool Production in the New River Basin. In *Hohokam Settlement and Economic Systems in the Central New River Drainage, Arizona*, edited by David E. Doyel and Mark D. Elson, pp. 521-564. Soil Systems Publications in Archaeology No. 4. Phoenix.

Howard, Ann Valdo
1989 Analysis of the Waddell Ceramic Assemblage. In *Settlement, Subsistence, and Specialization in the Northern Periphery: The Waddell Project*, edited by Margerie Green, pp. 473-642. Archaeological Consulting Services Cultural Resources Report No. 65, Vol. 1. Tempe.

Huckell, Bruce B.
1982 *The Distribution of Fluted Points in Arizona: A Review and Update*. Arizona State Museum Archaeological Series No. 145. Tucson.

Johnson, Maureen G.
1972 *Placer Gold Deposits of Arizona*. U.S. Geological Survey Bulletin No. 1355. U.S. Government Printing Office, Washington, D.C.

Kearney, Thomas H., and Robert H. Peebles
1964 *Arizona Flora*. 2nd ed. University of California Press, Berkeley.

Keepaz, Carole
1977 Contamination of Archaeological Deposits by Seeds of Modern Origin with Particular Reference to the Use of Flotation. *Journal of Archaeological Sciences* 4:221-229.

Keller, Donald R.
1984 *Gray Mountain, a Prehistoric Chert Source Site in Coconino County, Arizona*. The Arizona Archaeologist No. 19. Arizona Archaeological Society, Phoenix.

1986 *Archaeological Survey of the Mead to Phoenix 500 kV Direct Current Transmission Line Preferred Alternative*. 2 vols. Museum of Northern Arizona Department of Anthropology Project No. A-81-90. Flagstaff.

Kendrick, Grace
1963 *The Antique Bottle Collector*. Western Printing and Publishing, Sparks, Nevada.

Klein, Jeffrey, J. C. Lerman, P. E. Damon, and E. K. Ralph
1982 Calibration of Radiocarbon Dates: Tables Based on the Consensus Data of the Workshop on Calibrating the Radiocarbon Time Scale. *Radiocarbon* 24(2):103-150.

McClintock, James H.
1916 *Arizona*. vol 2. S. J. Clarke, Chicago.

Martin, Alexander C., and William D. Barkley
1973 *Seed Identification Manual*. University of California Press, Berkeley.

Minnis, Paul E.
1981 Seeds in Archaeological Sites: Sources and Some Interpretive Problems. *American Antiquity* 46(1):143-152.

Parker, Kitty F.
1972 *An Illustrated Guide to Arizona Weeds*. University of Arizona Press, Tucson.

Pilles, Peter J., Jr.
1981 A Review of Yavapai Archaeology. In *The Protohistoric Period in the North American Southwest, A.D. 1450-1700*, edited by David R. Wilcox and W. Bruce Masse, pp. 163-182. Arizona State University Anthropological Research Papers No. 24. Tempe.

Rankin, Adrianne G., and Keith L. Katzer
1989 Agricultural Systems in the ACS Waddell Project Area. In *Settlement, Subsistence, and Specialization in the Northern Periphery: The Waddell Project*, edited by Margerie Green, pp. 981-1020. Archaeological Consulting Services Cultural Resources Report No. 65. Tempe.

Rice, Glen E., and Edward Dobbins
1981 *Prehistoric Community Patterns in the Western Deserts of Arizona*. Arizona State University Anthropological Field Studies No. 2. Tempe.

Rock, James T.
1984 Cans in the Countryside. *Historical Archaeology* 18:97-111.

Rodgers, James B.
1987 *Studies along the Lower Agua Fria River: The Eastwing Site and the Marinette Canal*. Museum of Northern Arizona Research Paper No. 37. Flagstaff.

Ruppé, Patricia A.
1988 Analysis of the Macrobotanical Remains. In *Investigations of the Baccharis Site and Extension Arizona Canal*, edited by David H. Greenwald, pp. 140-159. Museum of Northern Arizona Research Paper No. 40. Flagstaff.

Russell, Frank
1908 *The Pima Indians*. Annual Report of the Bureau of American Ethnology No. 26. Smithsonian Institution, Washington, D.C.

Schaller, David M.
1985 Petrographic Analysis of Ground Stone Artifacts. In *Hohokam Settlement and Economic System in the Central New River Drainage, Arizona*, edited by David E. Doyel and Mark D. Elson, p 779-781. Soil Systems Publications in Archaeology No. 4. Phoenix.

Schoenwetter, James, and Larry Doerschlag
1971 Surficial Pollen Records from Central Arizona 1: Sonoran Desertshrub. *Journal of the Academy of Sciences* 6:216-221.

Schroeder, Albert H.
1974 *A Study of Yavapai History, Part II*. Garland, New York.

1975 *The Hohokam, Sinagua and the Hakataya*. I.V.C. Museum Society Occasional Paper No. 3. El Centro, California.

Sellers, William B., and Richard H. Hill (editors)
1974 *Arizona Climate 1931-1972*. University of Arizona Press, Tucson.

Simonis, Don
1988 Milk Can Chronology for Dating Historical Sites. Ms. on file, USDI Bureau of Land Management, Kingman, Arizona.

Sires, Earl W.
1984 Excavations at El Polvorón (AZ U:15:59). In *Hohokam Archaeology along the Salt-Gila Aqueduct, Central Arizona Project: Prehistoric Occupation of the Queen Creek Delta*, edited by Lynn S. Teague and Patricia L. Crown, pp. 219-354. Arizona State Museum Archaeological Series No. 150, Vol. 4. Tucson.

Spector, Janet Doris
1970 Seed Analysis in Archaeology. *The Wisconsin Archaeologist* 51:163-190.

Spoerl, Patricia M., and George J. Gumerman (editors)
1984 *Prehistoric Cultural Development in Central Arizona: Archaeology of the Upper New River Region*. Southern Illinois University Center for Archaeological Investigations Occasional Paper No. 5. Carbondale.

Stone, Connie L.
1986 *Deceptive Desolation: Prehistory of the Sonoran Desert in West Central Arizona*. USDI Bureau of Land Management Cultural Resource Series No. 1. Phoenix.

Szuter, Christine R.
1984 Faunal Exploitation and the Reliance on Small Animals among the Hohokam. In *Hohokam Archaeology along the Salt-Gila Aqueduct, Central Arizona Project: Environment and Subsistence*, edited by Lynn S. Teague and Patricia L. Crown, pp. 139-169. Arizona State Museum Archaeological Series No. 150, Vol. 7. The University of Arizona, Tucson.

Toulouse, Julian H.
1969 *Fruit Jars*. Thomas Nelson, Nashville.

1971 *Bottle Makers and Their Marks*. Thomas Nelson, Nashville.

Turner, Raymond M., and David E. Brown
1982 Sonoran Desertscrub. In *Desert Plants, Special Issue: Biotic Communities of the American Southwest, United States and Mexico*, vol. 4, nos. 1-4, edited by David E. Brown, pp. 181-222. University of Arizona Press, Tucson.

Vokes, Arthur W.
1988 Ceramics. In *The Fourmile Wash Project: Archaeological Excavations at Eight Sites in the Tonopah Desert, Western Arizona*, by Earl W. Sires, pp. 51-67. SWCA Anthropological Research Paper No. 1. Flagstaff and Tucson.

Weaver, Donald E., Jr.
1974 *Archaeological Investigations at the Westwing Site, AZ T:7:27(ASM), Agua Fria Valley, Arizona*. Arizona State University Anthropological Research Papers No. 7. Tempe.

1980 The Northern Frontier, Hohokam Regional Diversity as Seen from the Lower Salt River Valley. In *Current Issues in Hohokam Prehistory*, edited by E. David Doyel and Fred Plog, pp. 121-133. Arizona State University Anthropological Research Papers No. 23. Tempe.

Weber, Steven A., and P. David Seaman (editors)
1985 *Havasupai Habitat*. University of Arizona Press, Tucson.

Weed, Carol S.
1972 The Beardsley Canal Site. *The Kiva* 38(2):57-94.

Wilcox, David R., and Lynette O. Shenk
1977 *The Architecture of the Casa Grande and its Interpretation*. Arizona State Museum Archaeological Series No. 115. The University of Arizona, Tucson.

Wilcox, David R., and Charles Sternberg
1983 *Hohokam Ballcourts and their Interpretation*. Arizona State Museum Archaeological Series No. 160. The University of Arizona, Tucson.